WOMEN AND TRANQUILLISERS

CELIA HADDON has worked in Fleet Street for twenty years, and is one of its best-known women writers. She is also the author of *The Limits of Sex* (Michael Joseph) and co-author of *The Sunday Times Book of Body Maintenance* (Michael Joseph). She broadcasts frequently on radio, and has also appeared on television. She is married, and lives in London.

HEALTHCARE FOR WOMEN SERIES

Everything You Need to Know about the Pill
Wendy Cooper and Dr Tom Smith

Lifting the Curse
Beryl Kingston

Thrush
Caroline Clayton

Women and Depression
Deidre Sanders

Women's Problems: An A to Z
Dr Vernon Coleman

Women and Tranquillisers
Celia Haddon

WOMEN AND TRANQUILLISERS

Celia Haddon

SHELDON PRESS
LONDON

First published in Great Britain in 1984 by
Sheldon Press, SPCK, Marylebone Road, London NW1 4DU

British Library Cataloguing in Publication Data

Haddon, Celia
    Women and tranquillisers.—(Health for women)
    1. Benzodiazepines   2. Women—Drug use
    I. Title   II. Series
    615.'7882   RM666.B42
    ISBN 0–85969–420–8
    ISBN 0–85969–413–4 Pbk

Typeset by The Bocardo Press Ltd., Cowley, Oxford

Printed in Great Britain by
Richard Clay (The Chaucer Press) Ltd.
Bungay, Suffolk

Contents

Introduction by Professor Malcolm Lader   1

1. Tranquillisers and Sleeping Pills   4
2. Taking Pills Safely   15
3. Understanding the Risks   26
4. Becoming Dependent on Pills   37
5. Six Case Histories   49
6. How the Case Histories Got Better   57
7. Stopping Tranquillisers and Sleeping Pills   65
8. Living without Pills   78
9. Learning to Live with Anxiety   91
10. Dependence in Family and Friends   104

Appendix 1: Barbiturates   115
Appendix 2: Self-Help Groups   116
Index   119

Introduction

I am very pleased to have the opportunity to introduce this book by Celia Haddon to you. It contains useful, practical and sensible advice concerning tranquilliser withdrawal. Over the last few years we have become more aware and more and more concerned about the problem of dependence on tranquillisers prescribed by doctors. We have known for quite a time that if people push the dose of tranquillisers up and up then they will become dependent, and have major problems when they try to withdraw. What has crept up on the medical profession unannounced and unexpectedly is the discovery that problems can occur even when people have been taking their tranquillisers at the normal prescribed therapeutic dose, especially if they have done this for months or years. The extent of the problem is not known in detail, but I estimate that over 100000 people in the country would have full withdrawal problems if they were to stop their tranquilliser medication. This book, therefore, is most timely in setting out the problem and the background and, most important, in giving clear advice on how to deal with the practical difficulties.

The various types of drugs involved are explained, and information is given about what tranquillisers are, what they do and how to identify them. Because these drugs are such a commercial success, many pharmaceutical companies have rushed to introduce new members of the group which differ marginally from the original compounds, Librium and Valium. A large number now clutter up the market and, as some have several trade names, it is difficult to keep tabs on them all. It is also easy to confuse them with other drugs acting on the brain such as the major tranquillisers (antipsychotics) used in major psychiatric illnesses, and the antidepressants used to treat depression. Another area of confusion is the definition of dependence, addiction, tolerance, misuse, abuse – these are all matters of opinion even to experts such as World Health Organization committees who, often, can only agree to differ.

The problem of dependence on tranquillisers is particularly relevant to women as they take these drugs twice as much as men, and encounter dependence problems twice as much. Nevertheless, all the background information and the advice given is just as relevant to men as women. Some case histories are outlined, and these seem to me to be typical of the sort of problems that are met with. The problems of withdrawal are discussed, and keep a very good balance: it is not routinely easy to withdraw, nor is it so difficult that nobody succeeds. I cannot predict who will find major difficulties withdrawing and I am constantly amazed at the range and duration of the symptoms which occur.

To single out one part of the book for particular attention, I recommend Chapter 7 on the plan of action for withdrawal. If possible you should do this under the supervision of your own GP. Sadly, some doctors are still ignorant of the topic, or do not wish to face up to the problem of dependent patients. Consequently, self-help groups have been mushrooming all over the country and play an essential role in helping people. Withdrawing without supervision should only be the very last resort. Not only is a plan for withdrawal set in this book but sensible ways of coping with the general anxiety and stress of withdrawal are given. Finally, the help and advice to relatives is very important because they often have to help bear the burden of the problems encountered by patients.

Many people trying to withdraw become disheartened, but I believe that everyone is capable, with help, of stopping their tranquillisers. Much research is needed to find out why some people become dependent on tranquillisers while others do not. Much more detail is needed of what happens to the brain when drugs have been taken for year after year — as so often happens. One important question is whether a safe tranquilliser can ever be developed – a substance to lessen severe anxiety without inducing dependence. In answer to the question, 'do we need tranquillisers at all?', I believe that benefit is felt by a small number of people whose anxiety is so severe that it interferes with their everyday activities. For most people, however, tranquillisers should be used only in the short term, and those of you who have been taking them for a long time should seriously consider whether you are still benefiting. If the answer is no, I recommend Celia Haddon's book to inform you about anxiety and tranquillisers, and in particular to help you withdraw, preferably under medical supervision.

Professor Malcom Lader, 1984

ONE

Tranquillisers and Sleeping Pills

Since the beginning of medicine, women and men have gone to their doctors for help with their nerves. Doctors have tried to help them with various remedies, medicines and drugs. If a woman today asks her doctor for help with her nerves, she is likely to be given a tranquilliser.

Tranquillisers are among the most common drugs prescribed by doctors. Yet many people are muddled about which drugs actually are tranquillisers; they may think of them simply as 'nerve pills'. Sometimes doctors talk about 'sedatives' instead of tranquillisers. The drugs which are usually described as tranquillisers have many different names, and they come in tablets and capsules of many different colours.

The word 'tranquillisers' mainly applies to one family of drugs. Its chemical name is the benzodiazepines, and these drugs are also known as the 'minor tranquillisers'. They are called this because they are used for minor illnesses. But there are also some 'major tranquillisers', from different drug families, which are used for major mental illnesses. Minor tranquillisers are mostly prescribed by ordinary family doctors, for people who do not need hospital or specialized help.

This book is about the benzodiazepine minor tranquillisers. Most people will be familiar with some of the brand names of these drugs — names like Valium, Ativan and Librium. Tranquillisers of this kind are mainly taken by women who feel they need help in coping with feelings of anxiety.

The benzodiazepine family of drugs also includes drugs with names like Mogadon or Dalmane. These are given as sleeping pills. Doctors call them 'hypnotics', the medical word for sleeping pills, but most people do not realize that they are simply tranquillisers taken at night in larger doses. Just like tranquillisers they calm people down and get rid of anxiety, and this calming effect makes people go to sleep more easily. Everything in this book applies both to the benzodiazepine tranquillisers and to the benzodiazepine sleeping pills.

How many people take tranquillisers or sleeping pills?

The minor tranquillisers and sleeping pills are very popular drugs. About one in five women and one in ten men in Britain take a tranquilliser at some time during the year. About one in every forty adults takes these drugs daily every day of the year.

Indeed, these drugs are widely used all over the developed world. The Germans take about the same amount of tranquillisers as the British. In Belgium seventeen out of 100 people take these drugs, in Spain one in ten. In the United States, ten million Americans took tranquillisers in 1978, and Valium was the most widely prescribed drug from 1972 to 1980.

In both Britain and the United States twice as many women as men are given tranquillisers; Valium, Librium and Mogadon are probably the most widely known names. By now almost half the women in Britain have taken either a daytime tranquilliser or a sleeping pill at night at some point in their lives. Older women are more likely to be given tranquillisers than younger ones. Divorced and separated women are more likely to take them than single or married women.

In Britain, many people get their tranquillisers or sleeping pills on repeat prescriptions from their doctor. Quite often they do not have to see the doctor for a consultation; they just ring up and collect the prescription from the receptionist.

In hospitals sleeping pills are sometimes handed out as a matter of routine. A recent survey of old people's homes in Scotland showed that the elderly in these homes were getting more sleeping pills than old people living outside.

Many women and men have been on tranquillisers or sleeping pills not just for months, but for years. Some people take both sorts of pills. A recent survey showed that almost half the psychotropic drugs (those that include tranquillisers) given out by doctors had been first prescribed

5

two or more years ago. Three out of five repeat prescriptions had been obtained without seeing the doctor.

When were tranquillisers invented?

The benzodiazepine family of drugs was first invented in 1933, but nobody noticed they were important then. In the 1950s it was noticed that one of these drugs seemed to tame aggressive monkeys. The new tranquillisers were born.

The first tranquilliser on the market was Librium, which came into use at the beginning of the 1960s. It was followed by Valium. Then sleeping pills like Mogadon and Dalmane became common. Now there are many kinds of benzodiazepine tranquillisers and sleeping pills with many different brand names.

Until these new drugs arrived, the sedatives and sleeping pills mainly prescribed by doctors came from a family of drugs called the barbiturates. But today barbiturates are not often prescribed just as sedatives or sleeping pills. Occasionally women still take them, if they have been taking them for years. (For advice about barbiturates see Appendix 1, page 115).

Barbiturates had severe disadvantages. Although they were efficient in sedating people or making them sleep, they were also dangerous in overdose. Even a small overdose of barbiturates could be fatal. Besides, they were addictive. Once the new benzodiazepine drugs became available, they quickly took over from the barbiturates.

Why were doctors so enthusiastic about the new drugs?

The new benzodiazepines were much much safer than the barbiturates as far as overdoses were concerned. It was jokingly said that the only way to overdose an experimental guinea-pig to death with benzodiazepines was to bury it alive in tablets! People who took even a whole bottle of tranquillisers in a suicide attempt usually survived.

Quite rightly doctors started taking their patients off the barbiturates and putting them on to the new tranquillisers and sleeping pills. They thought of these pills as 'safe'.

And, of course, they *are* safe — from an overdose point of view.

Many doctors also thought that these new pills were 'safe' as far as addiction was concerned, and scientific papers sometimes declared that people would not usually become addicted to them.

Naturally, in the first few years, there was very little evidence that the drugs could cause problems in the long run. In the early years very few people had taken them for long periods. Besides, even with the barbiturates it took the best part of fifty years before doctors realized just how powerfully addictive they could be.

Tranquillisers and sleeping pills of the benzodiazepine family have not been on the market that long. So it is perhaps not surprising that it is only now that doctors are having second thoughts, and realizing that these drugs *are* addictive and should *not* be taken for months and years at a time.

Why doctors are unaware of this

Doctors find it difficult to keep up to date with all the most recent medical research. Thus many ordinary family doctors are still slow to realize that tranquillisers and sleeping pills should not be handed out lightly. Indeed, some doctors may even lose count of the repeat prescriptions for such drugs that they are signing.

One survey looked at the way doctors prescribed tranquillisers, sedatives, sleeping pills and antidepressants in Bath, in the West of England. One in ten of the patients receiving such drugs had been on them for more than ten years. 'The longer the patient had been taking the drug the longer it was since they had been seen by the doctor,' said the survey.

Doctors may simply lose track of their prescribing habits. One Derbyshire family doctor decided to keep a special record of all his consultations, by visit and by phone, for five weeks. He admitted that it was difficult to work out why some people got drugs and others did not.

He also admitted the women were more likely to be given drugs like tranquillisers than men were. 'My impression is that an anxious or depressed young man is less likely to get a psychotropic drug when coming to see me than a woman of the same age.'

Are you taking tranquillisers?

In the past week almost one in four people in Britain have taken some kind of medicine or tablets prescribed by their doctor. Some people take tablets almost every day. For instance, the contraceptive pill (the Pill as it is known) is taken daily.

Not everybody is sure what they are taking. Many women just think of their pills as 'my heart tablets', or 'my nerve pills'. Sometimes they are not even sure of the drug's name, and even if they know the name they are not sure what sort of drug it is.

It is very important, if you are using this book correctly, to discover exactly what pills you are taking. You can ask your doctor politely while he is writing out the prescription, and make a note of the name, if you are afraid you will forget it.

Sometimes doctors are too busy to talk, or do not like their patients to ask questions. In this case have a look at the prescription, as normally the name of the drug will be on it. If you cannot read the handwriting, ask the pharmacist for the name when you hand over the prescription. Pharmacists are sometimes easier to talk to than doctors.

It is well worth your while to write down the name, as soon as the doctor or pharmacist tells you. Also ask him what strength the tablets or capsules are. The strength of a drug comes in so many milligrams (mg) per tablet, a milligram being a thousandth of a gram (g), or in even smaller measures called micrograms (μ).

This information should also normally be on the bottle that you get from the pharmacist. Usually a bottle of pills has the name of the drug, the strength of the tablets, and when they are to be taken. Occasionally a doctor will ask the pharmacist to leave off the name, but this is unusual.

Tranquillisers and sleeping pills — international and brand names

The various tablets have a rather confusing variety of names.

Each drug has an internationally approved name. Some tablets also have a brand name — a name invented by the company which makes the drug.

For instance, Valium is a well-known brand name for a drug which is internationally known as diazepam. Sometimes, if the doctor is prescribing the cheapest sort of diazepam, it will not have a brand name at all. The bottle will simple say 'diazepam' or 'diazepam BP'. The most common brand name for diazepam is Valium; but there are many other brand names — Alupram, Atensine, Evacalm, Solis, Stesolid, Tensium and Valrelease.

New versions of tranquillisers and sleeping pills come out almost every year. You can check the name of your pills against the list in this book (pages 9 and 10), which was compiled in 1983. If you think you may have a new kind of tranquilliser, introduced after that date, ask the pharmacist for advice, or look it up in the British National Formulary, with the help of your local reference library.

Long-acting tranquillisers

International name	*Brand name(s)*
Bromazepam	Lexotan
Chlordiazepoxide	Librium, Tropium
Clobazam	Frisium
Clorazepate dipotassium	Tranxene
Diazepam	Alupram, Atensine, Evacalm, Solis, Stesolid, Tensium, Valium and Valrelease
Ketazolam	Anxon
Medazepam	Nobrium
Prazepam	Centrax

Medium-acting tranquillisers

International name	*Brand name(s)*
Alprazolam	Xanax
Lorazepam	Almazine, Ativan
Oxazepam	Serenid-D, Serenid Forte

Long-acting sleeping pills

International name	*Brand name(s)*
Flunitrazepam	Rohypnol
Flurazepam	Dalmane
Nitrazepam	Mogadon, Nitrados, Remnos, Somnite, Surem, and Unisomnia

Medium-acting sleeping pills

International name	*Brand name(s)*
Lormetazepam	Noctamid
Temazepam	Euhypnos, Euhypnos Forte, Normison

Short-acting sleeping pills

International name	*Brand name(s)*
Triazolam	Halcion

There is also a benzodiazepine drug which is used to sedate people before an operation, or used with local anaesthetics. Its international name is midazolam, and its brand name is Hypnovel. For the treatment of epilepsy there is a benzodiazepine with the international name of clonazepam (brand name Rivotril).

If your prescription has none of these names on it, and is not for a drug introduced since 1983, then you are *not* taking a minor tranquilliser. Sometimes doctors prescribe anti-depressants or small doses of major tranquillisers or give non-benzodiazepine sedatives. *The advice in this book applies only to the benzodiazepine tranquillisers and sleeping pills.*

How tranquillisers and sleeping pills work

These pills influence the neurotransmitters, the chemical messengers which convey impulses between nerves in the brain. They dampen down nervous activity throughout the brain. This produces a better mood, and has a relaxing effect on the muscles. It also makes people less alert.

The person taking the drug *feels* calmer. But these pills do *not* cure anxiety, or have a curative effect on the nerves. All they do is alter the mood of the person taking them.

Benzodiazepine sleeping pills have a similar effect. They help people drop off to sleep, but the sleep that follows is not quite the same as natural slumber.

There are four stages of natural sleep — the first stage is that drowsy feeling which occurs around the time we drop off. The second stage is definite unconsciousness, followed by medium deep sleep at the third stage, and deep slumber at the fourth stage, when the activity of the brain is at its lowest.

At various times during the night there are also bursts of what is called REM sleep — sleep during which there is rapid eye movement. The brain activity and the eye movements of the sleeper resemble those of an awake person who is looking round at things. At this time the brain is creating fantasies and the sleeper is usually dreaming.

People need the deep sleep of stages three and four, if they are to feel properly rested the following day. They also need REM sleep. Without this, they feel irritable and aggressive.

Benzodiazepine sleeping pills interfere with REM sleep — though not nearly as much as barbiturate sleeping pills do. They also seem to lessen the amount of stage three and stage four sleep that people get. Women or men taking these sleeping pills will not be getting quite the same kind of slumber that they would get without a pill.

Tranquilliser and sleeping pill hangovers

Some of the tranquillisers and sleeping pills last much longer than others. The long-acting kind last up to twenty-four hours or longer, while the short-acting kind last for only a few hours.

The long-acting pills are therefore usually prescribed only once a day, while the short-acting or medium-acting tranquillisers must be taken two or three times a day.

This difference is particularly important with sleeping pills. The long-acting sleeping pills last right into the following day, giving the same effect as taking a daytime tranquilliser. Shorter-acting sleeping pills have less of a morning hangover effect.

Why are tranquillisers prescribed?

Tranquillisers should be prescribed for anxiety. Some common anxiety symptoms are worrying thoughts that will not go away; fear and apprehension; irritation and quick temper; anxiety about the future. Bodily symptoms include heart palpitations, diarrhoea, trembling, fainting, stomach upset, urge to urinate, and sweating.

Most anxiety attacks do not last for more than about eight weeks. With or without pills, the anxiety diminishes. Tranquillisers are useful for people whose anxiety is so severe that it interferes with their normal life. They just cannot cope because of their anxious feelings.

Anxiety is one of the reasons why people find it difficult to get to sleep. When they lie awake in bed, they find worrying thoughts and fears come into their minds and will not go away. Their bodies will not relax.

Benzodiazepine drugs are also used in other ways. Sometimes they are given in an intravenous injection before dental treatment or minor medical treatment. They are given as muscle-relaxants to people suffering from slipped discs and strained muscles, and also prescribed for some types of epilepsy.

What tranquillisers cannot do for people

Unfortunately tranquillisers are also prescribed for conditions that they cannot truly help. Some doctors are convinced that they are such safe pills that they may give them out far too freely.

Tranquillisers alone should not be prescribed for depression
Benzodiazepines are 'downers', meaning that they depress the central nervous system. People who are already depressed will probably feel worse if they are prescribed just tranquillisers on their own. If your doctor tries to give you tranquillisers only for depression, tell him you would prefer antidepressants.

Sometimes doctors prescribe tranquillisers together with antidepressants. This makes sense, if the patient has been feeling both depressed *and* anxious. The theory is that the antidepressants will work on the depression, and the tranquillisers will work on the anxiety.

If you are feeling depressed, *without* feeling anxious, it is probably still best just to take antidepressants on their own. There is just a possibility that the 'downer' effect of the tranquillisers will make the antidepressants less effective.

Tranquillisers should not be prescribed for everyday anxiety
Ordinary anxiety does not need pills. It is quite normal to feel anxious occasionally. Taking pills to deal with it is like using a sledge-hammer to crack a nut.

Sleeping pills should not be prescribed for early morning waking
People who wake early in the morning are often suffering from depression. Taking benzodiazepine sleeping pills will only make the depression worse.

Are these drugs really worthwhile?

Until recently doctors and ordinary people have been too enthusiastic about these drugs. Now the pendulum has begun to swing in the other direction. A few people are beginning to feel violently opposed to them.

Tranquillisers and their sleeping pill cousins are extremely useful drugs. They can help millions of people through their temporary panic or sleeplessness. And thanks to these drugs, doctors are now prescribing far fewer dangerous barbiturates.

The dangers and disadvantages of benzodiazepine drugs have arisen mainly because doctors have prescribed them too freely and patients have demanded pills to cope with conditions that did not need pills. There isn't a pill for every problem.

Doctors badly need educating about the risks of over-enthusiastic prescribing. They need to be more careful about issuing repeat prescriptions or giving people these drugs on the slightest demand.

13

Ordinary women need more information too. If women know more about the risks of these drugs, they will be less likely to demand pills from their doctor. They will also be better placed to understand how tranquillisers and sleeping pills should be taken.

This book tells you when tranquillisers and sleeping pills will be useful, how to take them safely, and how to avoid becoming dependent on them. For those women who have been taking these pills for years in good faith, it offers a survival guide on how to stop taking them and learn to live without them.

TWO

Taking Pills Safely

One of the mysteries of the way tranquillisers are so widely prescribed is why women, rather than men, seem to be given these pills more often. Is it that women are more likely to need these drugs? Do they ask for them more insistently? Or is it that doctors think women need them more often, even if they do not?

The answers to these questions are not clear cut. In almost every developed country in the west more women than men take tranquillisers. In Britain the proportion is two to one. The reason may partly be the doctor's idea that women are more likely to need such drugs. It is significant that many of the tranquilliser advertisements in medical journals show women patients rather than men.

A survey in 1974 showed that the women who were given these pills were likely to be between twenty-five to thirty-four, the age when they are looking after young children, and between forty-five to fifty-four, the age when children have left home. A quarter of the women had come to the doctor complaining of pain, but in only one case did the doctor actually diagnose pain. A number of women who had not complained of depression were nevertheless diagnosed as depressed.

The pattern in which the drugs were prescribed has several odd features. Various studies in western countries show that married women receive twice as many prescriptions than their single sisters. One American survey showed that working women were less likely to be taking tranquillisers and similar drugs than housewives who stayed at home.

However, it is also true that women are more likely to suffer from anxiety than men. A whole series of surveys have been carried out which asked people whether they suffered from emotional disturbances of what the researchers called 'psychic distress'. More women than men reported this. Thus the greater use of tranquillisers by women may reflect this greater emotional trouble in the first place.

In some ways, women's lives have more stressful moments than men. Women, if they are married, are rarely independent of their partners financially. Even if she does work, the married woman is unlikely to be the major bread-winner. The non-working wife is likely to be entirely financially dependent upon her husband.

Just as women give up their surnames on marriage and take their husbands', so they are likely to take their status and position in life from their menfolk. Research has shown that women have to make a greater adjustment in marriage than men. Even in equal marriages, where both have careers, women are still more likely to do the bulk of household chores.

Men have stresses and strains in life. They face money worries, unemployment, redundancy, changes of job, and bereavements. Women, through their husbands, are likely to be affected by these as well. Women also face the stress of changing roles through their life — from independent women to dependent wife, from childless wife to mother, from mother to the time when children have fled the nest.

At moments of crisis, particularly times when there is not much action that can be taken to solve problems, people are likely to feel anxiety. It could be argued that women have more potential life changes to face, and may be more prone to anxiety on this account.

These are all reasons which may explain why women, rather than men, are more likely to take tranquillisers. But they are not necessarily justifications for this. Feminists have argued that much is wrong with a society where about one in twenty women have to be doped to get through their daily life. Even women who are not at all in favour of women's liberation are often worried by the thought that so many of their sisters need pills.

The pill society

Since the medical advances of the last fifty to 100 years, most of us have become used to the idea that drugs can cure illnesses. Indeed, drugs like antibiotics have saved literally millions from death. Drugs which act on the mind have also kept many people from having to go into psychiatric hospitals.

The result is that many people feel that getting over an emotional problem requires a pill. One young family doctor started his general practice determined not to hand out tranquillisers too freely. He offered patients a chance to talk to him, rather than simply a prescription.

'In the short time I've been in general practice, I've felt terribly pressurized into prescribing these drugs,' he admitted a year later. 'When I tell people that pills won't help, I offer to talk to them about it. They reply: "Talking won't help. I need my pills."'

A group practice in the Ealing area of London discovered much the same response in 1980, when the three partners decided that they would be more careful about prescribing tranquillisers and sleeping pills.

The doctors reported:

> Many patients agreed with our new policy in general, but they claimed to be a special case and begged to be excluded from our programme. By agreement all the partners were equally firm and from March to October 1980, 251 long-term or occasional users of benzodiazepines were identified and withdrawn from these drugs. About eight to ten patients left the practice on account of this policy . . .

Popping in a pill to deal with moments of stress is now considered quite respectable. One woman newspaper columnist in 1982 was blithely recommending borrowing a Valium whenever needed. 'I would say that most women I know keep some "Vallies" in their handbag. It is worth remembering that, if you ever have to endure the horror of being stuck in an underground train or a lift, there will almost certainly be a woman around with a Valium.'

In this climate of opinion, it is no wonder that thousands, even millions, of women turn to tranquillisers and sleeping pills to help them cope. Yet, if they knew the whole truth of these drugs, some of them might decide against ever taking them.

Should I take tranquillisers?

It would be foolish and cruel to say that women should

17

never take tranquillisers or sleeping pills. The benzodiazepine family of drugs are very helpful to many — when they are used sparingly and correctly. Any woman who is already taking these drugs should only stop after taking her doctor's advice first.

But like all drugs, tranquillisers and sleeping pills are not an entirely safe cure-all. They have side-effects. When we think of side-effects and drugs, we probably think of horrifying scare stories about drugs that kill or drugs like thalidomide that maim. In fact, almost every drug has side-effects. Even aspirin, which is freely sold over the counter, has risks. The alcohol we drink can be dangerous. Even the caffeine in our coffee is a drug which has some side-effects.

The benzodiazepine drugs are not dangerous, *if* they are used correctly. But they are often *not* used correctly. Sometimes doctors forget to tell women about the side-effects. Sometimes the women taking the pills forget the doctor's advice. Sometimes even doctors may not be clear in their own minds about how these drugs should be used.

Any kind of medicine or pill should be treated with caution. It is always a question of balancing up the risks and the benefits. Most doctors do this when they prescribe drugs. But if their women patients were better informed, they could play their part in making sure these pills are used correctly.

Tranquillisers only have a temporary effect

Perhaps the most important single fact to remember is that tranquillisers only work for a few months. The first four to six weeks will see improvement, but after that the effect will level off. Nobody has proved that tranquillisers do much for people after four months' use.

However, this temporary effect is what most people need. Anxiety and panic attacks usually disappear anyway in about two months, even without pills. Most people, therefore, will not need to take tranquillisers any longer. But those women who have severe and persistent anxiety will find that tranquillisers only take away their anxiety for a few weeks. Even so this temporary break from anxiety may be a considerable relief. This temporary effect of tranquillisers means that people who are taking the pills for anxiety should not be on them for months at a time. After six months tranquillisers will not be doing *anything* for anxiety; they have become unnecessary and ineffective.

What tranquillisers do seem to continue to do, however, is somehow to take the sharp edge off life, and blur out some of the reality. Women who feel that they still *need* their drug for anxiety, after six months has past, may have become dependent on the drug. The feeling of needing a pill is not proof that the pill is actually doing you good.

In Britain, there is a Government Committee on the Review of Medicines, with experts whose job it is to report on the safety and effectiveness of drugs. In 1980, they reported on the benzodiazepine drugs and their findings came as a surprise to many doctors with patients who had been taking these drugs for years.

The committee further agreed with an American study which had carried out many laboratory investigations into sleeping pills. These studies 'show that most hypnotics tend to lose their sleep-promoting properties within three to fourteen days of continuous use. The committee further noted that there was little convincing evidence that benzo-diazepines were efficacious in the treatment of anxiety after four months' continuous treatment.'

In other words, most sleeping pills are useless after three to fourteen days. Tranquillisers are probably no good for anxiety after four months.

In America, the authorities are in agreement. The Food and Drug Administration (FDA) has warned doctors to make sure that their prescriptions are only short-term ones, and that patients take the drugs correctly.

Tranquillisers and sleeping pills are interchangeable

Women who take a tranquilliser during the day and a sleeping pill at night would be surprised to discover that they could simply swap the pills around, although the names of the various drugs look very different indeed — Valium, Librium and Tranxene for day; Mogadon, Dalmane and Halcion at night.

Nevertheless the Committee on the Review of Medicines thought otherwise. It concluded that the way the benzodiazepine drugs were rigidly divided up into tranquillisers and sleeping pills 'did not appear to be based on the known pharmacological or clinical properties of this group of compounds'.

In other words, drugs like Mogadon could be taken as a daytime tranquilliser, and drugs like Valium could be taken as a night-time sleeping pill. The difference between them had more to do with the names they were given, and the way the drug companies advertised them, than with how they worked.

This underlines the fact that sleeping pills are really just like tranquillisers. Women who say: 'Oh, I'm not on tranquillisers, I just take a sleeping pill at night', are making a mistake. Taking a sleeping pill is just the same as taking a tranquilliser at night.

Thus, if you need to think about how much of these drugs you are taking, you must take into account both daytime tranquillisers and night-time sleeping pills. Unfortunately, it is not just a question of adding up the number of milligrams of both drugs. Benzodiazepine drugs come in very different potencies. With some drugs just a few milligrams have a powerful effect; with others the same effect has to be obtained by a large number of milligrams. Details of the different doses for the different pills can be found on page 25.

Thanks to the Committee's report we now know much more about how these drugs should be taken. There are three important rules for anyone thinking of taking them.

1. *Do not take them unless you need them*
This applies to all medicines, even aspirins. But sometimes tranquillisers and sleeping pills have been handed out so freely that people need reminding about this.

Tranquillisers should not be taken for ordinary day-to-day anxiety. In 1980 the American Food and Drug Commissioner, Jere E. Goyan, said:

> Tranquillisers can do a great good in helping people get through crisis situations or in helping with problems of mental illness.

20

Yet millions of Americans are taking them habitually just to deal with the anxiety of living . . . . These drugs were not intended to deal with normal anxiety.

In the United States the drug companies have agreed to advise doctors that their drugs are not for 'everyday' stress.

Some anxiety during everyday life is quite normal. It is normal to feel anxious about a dentist's appointment, an examination, a job interview, or a forthcoming driving test. The anxiety is part of the human body keying itself up for the event.

You should only consider taking pills, therefore, if your anxiety is so intense that it is interfering with the way you lead your daily life. Normally people manage to live through anxiety without being too severely affected by it.

Similarly, you should only take sleeping pills as a last resort. Later in the book (on page 101) there will be some suggestions on how to get a better night's rest without taking pills. Try these before you ask your doctor for sleeping pills.

2. *Take as small a dose as possible*
If you decide that you need a tranquilliser or a sleeping pill to cope with life for a little while, then ask your doctor for the smallest possible dose. If this does not seem to work, then you can go back to him and ask for more.

The doses for different drugs vary. As a general rule nobody should be on a total dose of more than fifteen milligrams (mg) of diazepam (Valium) a day, or thirty milligrams (mg) if the original anxiety was particularly severe. Normal doses for the other drugs can be found on page 25. Unfortunately people do move on to higher doses when they have been on the drugs for a long time. The dose edges upwards without either the patient or the doctor realizing the significance of it.

If you are already taking one kind of drug, say a sleeping pill, always remind your doctor about it *before* he prescribes tranquillisers. Indeed you should tell him about any other medicine you are taking as sometimes family doctors lose count of the amount and kind of pills people are on.

21

3. Take the pills for as short a time as possible

Taking either tranquillisers or sleeping pills daily for months on end has its dangers. The shorter the period you take them for the better. So aim to take them for weeks, not months.

As far as tranquillisers are concerned, the major improvement will come in the first four to six weeks. After that, though improvement may be maintained, there will be no further progress. After four months (as mentioned above), there is no proof that the pills will do you any good at all.

Plan to take the pills for only two weeks at first. If necessary try a further two weeks. The sooner you stop the pills the less risk there is of dependence upon them.

With sleeping pills it is not a good idea to take them continuously night after night. There is some evidence that lormetazepam and nitrazepam, and possibly some of the other benzodiazepines, have a longer-lasting effect — but most sleeping pills stay effective for only three to fourteen days.

It is much more sensible – if you must take sleeping pills — to take them intermittently, never more than three nights continuously. Use them to break a pattern of insomnia, then leave them aside for as long as possible.

If you decide to take tranquillisers or sleeping pills, or both, then you need safety guidelines for taking them. Unfortunately some doctors are too busy to warn patients of the side-effects of these drugs. Here is a twelve-point safety plan for the proper use of tranquillisers and sleeping pills.

The tranquilliser twelve-point safety plan

1. Do not take these drugs unless you seriously need them.

2. Take as small a dose as possible.

3. Take them for as short a time as possible. Use sleeping pills intermittently rather than continuously.

4. Never increase the dosage except by explicit orders from your doctor. Taking more than the dose he recommends is *dangerous*.

5. Never lend your pills. Never borrow pills from others.

6. When the doctor prescribes these pills, remind him of any other medicines or drugs you are taking — even drugs bought over the counter.

7. Do not drink more than one small measure of spirits, half a pint of beer or a small glass of wine within twenty-four hours of taking these drugs. This applies to sleeping pills as well as tranquillisers. There are *no* exceptions to this rule.

8. Do not drive during the first two weeks that you take either tranquillisers or sleeping pills. Do not operate heavy or dangerous machinery of any kind during the same period. If after two weeks you feel the pills are affecting your concentration, continue this ban.

9. Do not ask your doctor for repeat prescriptions.

10. Do not take tranquillisers or sleeping pills if you have been prescribed Tagamet for ulcers, or Antabuse for alcoholism.

11. If, when you start taking these pills, you find yourself becoming irritable, more anxious, aggressive or angry, go back and tell your doctor. Some tranquillisers make some people aggressive and angry rather than serene. Some individuals even feel *more* anxious on pills, rather than less.

12. If you are taking tranquillisers or sleeping pills, do not take antihistamines or any other mood-altering drug. This includes legal drugs like travel sickness pills, antidepressants (unless your doctor has specially put you on antidepressants and tranquillisers combined), and some epilepsy drugs. It also includes illegal drugs like cannabis or 'pot', and the so-called hard drugs including cocaine.

People who should not take tranquillisers or sleeping pills

Some people should not take these pills *at all*, except at times of grave medical need. These include:

1. *Pregnant women or women who might get pregnant*. The only safe way to make sure your unborn child does not suffer is not to take drugs of *any* kind during pregnancy.

23

The dangers from tranquillisers and sleeping pills are greatest in the first three months and last three months of pregnancy.

Any woman who is planning to get pregnant or is at risk of pregnancy should come off tranquillisers immediately. Drugs can harm the unborn child even before the woman knows for certain she is pregnant.

2. *Nursing women*. Tranquillisers and sleeping pills pass through the mother's milk and can harm the baby, who becomes sleepy and sucks poorly.

3. *The very elderly*. After the age of eighty old people should not be on these pills. Even sleeping pills can make them confused. After the age of sixty people should be on half doses of both tranquillisers and sleeping pills. Check this with the dosage chart on page 25.

4.*Heavy drinkers*. The drink limit in the twelve-point safety plan must be kept at all times every day. Heavy drinkers who may not always be able to keep it should not take these pills.

5. *People with a history of alcoholism, alcohol abuse, drug addiction or drug abuse*. These people may starting abusing tranquillisers, or may be more likely to develop a dependence on them.

Sometimes tranquillisers are used to help people get through the withdrawal symptoms of alcoholism or drug addiction. If doctors thoroughly understand addiction and alcoholism, and can *make sure* the patient is not drinking or taking drugs at the same time, the benzodiazepine drugs are helpful. Unfortunately, some doctors prescribe them not understanding that the alcoholic or addict may continue to drink or take drugs. *This practice is dangerous*.

Even recovered alcoholics and addicts — women and men who have maintained a life free from alcohol and drugs for many years — must be particularly careful about taking these drugs, and they should avoid mood-altering chemicals if possible.

Dosage Chart

These charts have been compiled from the British National Formulary (BNF), which gives doctors advice on the right dose for drugs of all kinds. Most doses are given in milligrams (abbreviated mg), but drugs which need small doses may be given in micrograms (abbreviated µg). There are 1000 micrograms to 1 milligram.

Tranquillisers

Name of drug	Normal daily dose	Dose for severe anxiety	Dose for elderly patient
Alprazolam	250–500 µg three times daily	total 3 mg during a day	250 µg three times daily
Bromazepam	1.5–6 mg three times daily	6–12 mg three times daily	should not be given to the elderly
Chlordiazepoxide	10 mg three times daily	total of 100 mg a day	
Clobazam	20–30 mg as daily total		
Clorazepate dipotassium	7.5–22.5 mg as daily total		
Diazepam	2 mg three times daily	total of 15–30 mg daily	
Ketazolam	15–60 mg as daily total		15 mg as a daily total
Lorazepam	1–4 mg as daily total	up to 10 mg as daily total	
Medazepam	5 mg twice or three times daily	up to 40 mg as a daily total	
Oxazepam	15–30 mg three to four times daily	up to 60 mg three times daily	10–20 mg three to four times daily
Prazepam	5–60 mg as daily total		15 mg as daily total

Note: Where the total dose is given, it will often be prescribed in divided doses during the day. Thus, for example, the daily total of prazepam is up to 60 mg, which might be administered in three doses of 20 mg. Some drugs can be given in higher doses for severe anxiety. Where no higher dose is mentioned, the ordinary dose must be taken as the maximum. As a general rule, if no specific dose is mentioned, patients over sixty should be on half the ordinary daily dose.

Sleeping pills

Name of drug	Normal dose	Dose for severe insomnia	Dose for elderly patient
Flunitrazepam	0.5–1 mg	1–2 mg	500 µg
Flurazepam	15–30 mg		15 mg
Lormetazepam	1 mg		500 µg
Nitrazepam	5–10 mg		2.5–5 mg
Temazepam	10–30 mg	up to 60 mg	5–15 mg
Triazolam	125–250 µg		125 µg

THREE

Understanding the Risks

Tranquillisers and sleeping pills are some of the safest drugs used in medicine today. That is why doctors have used them so widely and so enthusiastically. But taking any drug is always a question of balancing benefits against risks.

No drug is completely safe. There are many mild drugs in daily use which have considerable dangers. Tobacco is one — it is only mildly stimulating in its effects but it carries considerable risks to health. Alcohol is another drug in daily use which has potentially severe dangers. Even aspirin has side-effects that can be harmful to health.

Most ordinary people probably do not think of side-effects when they smoke their cigarettes, have a pint of beer, or take a couple of aspirins. Yet it might be better if they sometimes did. If you know the potential risks of a drug, then you are in a better position to decide whether to use it or not.

This is the reason for the twelve-point safety plan in the previous chapter. Many people taking tranquillisers may have been rather confused, perhaps even surprised, by some of the recommendations. It is easy to forget what the doctor said once you have come out of the surgery. Some doctors forget to warn their patients of the possible side-effects.

Common side-effects of tranquillisers and sleeping pills

Every medicine prescribed in Britain has an information sheet which tells doctors of its side-effects. This sheet can be found in a book call the *Data Sheet Compendium*, which is revised every fifteen months or so by the drug companies.

The guidelines for tranquillisers and sleeping pills were drawn up by the Committee on the Review of Medicines. They include this paragraph: 'Common adverse effects include drowsiness, sedation, blurring of vision, unsteadiness, and ataxia [loss of muscle coordination]. These effects occur following a single as well as repeated dosage and may persist well into the following day. Performance at skilled tasks and alertness may be impaired.'

In other words, the way people function in ordinary life may be affected — those taking these pills may feel sleepy, sometimes cannot see clearly, become unsteady on their feet, and lose muscular coordination.

These side-effects are not surprising. After all, tranquillisers are meant to sedate people, to relax them and calm them down. Indeed doctors sometimes give a single high dose of a tranquilliser to make people sleepy if they are dangerously excitable or overwrought.

On the whole, there is nothing to worry about with these particular side-effects. It is simply a question of being sensible, and not expecting to be particularly alert after taking the pills.

The higher the dose given, the more likely are such side-effects, which is one reason for taking as small a dose as is effective. Individuals vary a great deal in their susceptibility to drugs. Thus some people will feel very sleepy after tranquillisers; others may not notice much difference.

A side-effect of taking a long-lasting sleeping pill is that you are likely to feel rather drowsy the following morning and perhaps throughout the rest of the day.

Side-effects like this are most likely to occur in the first couple of weeks of taking the drug. After that time the body often adjusts to the drug, and these die down. Smokers may need higher doses of tranquillisers because tobacco counteracts the effects of these drugs.

If on the other hand, tranquillisers or sleeping pills slow you down too much, and these side-effects are severe, you probably need a smaller dose. Go back to your doctor and ask for tablets of a weaker strength.

Tranquillisers and driving

Most people do not realize that both tranquillisers and sleeping pills can affect your driving safety. Nearly everybody is familiar with the idea that we should not drink and drive. Even somebody who has had only two or three drinks may be dangerous on the road. Yet many people are surprised to discover that tranquillisers can also affect driving skill.

Naturally if you feel the side-effects of tranquillisers like drowsiness, blurred vision and loss of coordination, your eyesight, driving coordination and concentration will be affected, and you are not likely to drive well.

But tranquillisers and sleeping pills can affect how you drive even when you do not notice these side-effects. People who take sleeping pills may not even have realized that these pills continue working in the body the following day. and they continue to drive without knowing the risks.

Though much research has been done on drinking and driving, comparatively little has been done on tranquillisers and sleeping pills and driving. Recently, however, twelve women were given pills to take at night, then asked to drive over a test course the following day.

Four of the women were given flurazepam (Dalmane), a long-acting sleeping pill; four were given temazepam (Euhypnos), a shorter-acting pill; four were given a sugar pill (placebo) which contained no drug at all.

The women who had taken the real sleeping pills drove less well than those who had taken just the sugar pills. One of the tests was to drive round plastic bollards and in this test women who had taken the long-acting sleeping pill hit most bollards. The other test involved driving through gaps, and even the women who had been taking the short-acting pills made more mistakes than the women who had only taken the sugar pills.

The fact that the long-acting sleeping pills affected the women's driving ability the morning after did not surprise the researchers. But they were surprised that even the short-acting pill did so: 'We suggest . . . that doctors should advise patients to avoid morning driving for the first few days of taking one of these hypnotics (sleeping pills)'.

There have also been other studies which suggest that people taking tranquillisers are at greater risk of a road accident than people on no drugs at all. One small survey showed that those on such drugs had more than four times the risk of an accident than those on no drugs at all.

These findings are still controversial. It has been argued that perhaps people who need to take tranquillisers are more likely to be accident prone than those who do not need these pills. More research is needed.

Unfortunately nobody has yet done an experiment which tested *all* the different sorts of tranquillisers and sleeping pills and their effects on driving, as they may vary considerably. In one study, lorazepam (Ativan) seemed far more likely to affect people's driving skills than, for instance, clobazam (Frisium).

Ordinary women cannot wait until the scientists stop arguing before taking precautions with these pills. So to be on the safe side, it is wisest not to drive for the first two weeks of taking any of these pills — and *never* to drive if they make you feel sleepy, uncoordinated, or lacking in concentration.

This advice also applies to using all other heavy or somewhat dangerous machinery. If you operate potentially dangerous machinery at work, ask to be changed to a different job for the first fortnight of these pills. Avoid doing do-it-yourself tasks with drills, saws and other sharp tools during this period. Do not cut hedges or mow the lawn, if you feel any side-effects.

Tranquillisers and mental side-effects

The researchers who were testing clobazam and lorazepam and driving skills also looked at other mental activities. Both drugs affected women's ability with mental arithmetic. In addition, lorazepam (Ativan) also affected the women's ability to do very repetitive easy sums.

Once again more research is needed. But it looks as if tranquillisers and sleeping pills can affect women's ability both to learn and to remember things. This is not to say, of course, that the pills will turn a patient into a complete idiot!But they may affect the way you function. What you already know and have learned before taking pills will stay with you. An historian or a brain surgeon will not forget all her professional knowledge and expertise. But her daily work may be affected. Though she remembers what she already knows, she may forget things told her during the day. She may find it difficult to concentrate on repetitive and easy tasks, and her thinking may slow down slightly.

The consequences of this are very important. Suppose a woman is promoted at work, then finds she is terribly anxious about her new job. She is tense all day and lies awake worrying.

Tranquillisers or sleeping pills will calm her down and make her feel less anxious. She may *feel* more able to cope. But will this actually be so? If the pills make her forgetful and slow, her work may not improve. She will *feel* able to cope, but in fact be *less* able than she used to be.

The decision whether to take these pills is an individual one. The woman who has been promoted will have to decide whether the benefits of being less anxious outweigh the risks of perhaps not being so efficient at work.

Pills and the housewife

Women who are staying at home and looking after a family are engaged in very important work. Yet sometimes male doctors may feel that it does not matter if a housewife gets a bit drowsy or forgetful; they are, of course, quite wrong.

The decision on whether or not to take tranquillisers is just as vital for the housewife as it is for the working woman. She may find that pills help her by reducing her anxiety, so that she can better care for her children and the house.

On the other hand, just like the working woman, she may find herself forgetful, clumsy, or unable to concentrate. This matters just as much in the home as it does in an office. A woman who is badly affected by these pills may have accidents in the house, or not be alert enough to look after her children properly.

Besides, a housewife's self-esteem matters. The woman who forgets to pay the milkman, or cannot do simple household tasks because of lack of concentration, will feel extremely badly about it.

Once again, it is for the individual to weigh up the benefits and the risks of the pills. Being a good mother and a good housewife requires the best in people, just as having an outside job does.

Pills and pregnancy

Women have a special reason to be careful about taking any kind of pills or medicines. If they become pregnant, what they are taking into their bodies can affect the future of their unborn baby. It is now known that the first three months of pregnancy, a time before the woman herself may be sure that she is pregnant, is a period when the unborn child is particularly vulnerable.

As long ago as 1976, the American Food and Drug Administration warned that tranquillisers and sleeping pills should be avoided by women during the first three months of pregnancy. Women who taken them during this time may have a higher risk of giving birth to a baby with a cleft lip, for example.

'The studies do not demonstrate conclusively that these drugs, taken during early pregnancy, can cause cleft lip or other birth defects. But use of these tranquillisers during pregnancy is rarely a matter of urgency, and their use during this time should almost always be avoided,' said Alexander M. Schmidt, MD, the then Commissioner of Food and Drugs.

Once again ordinary women cannot wait till scientists agree on what is proven before taking precautions. Therefore the safe way to treat these drugs is to make sure they are *not* taken during pregnancy. But this advice is sometimes easier to give than to follow. How is a woman going to know she is pregnant in time? Should she wait until she has a pregnancy test before stopping these pills?

The safest way is to stop these pills *before* the baby is conceived. In America, this kind of precaution is called 'preconceptual planning'. All pills and medicines are ceased before contraception is stopped. In Britain there is now an organization which helps people practise 'preconceptual care' (see Appendix 2, page 116).

Women who are having sexual intercourse without contraception should therefore be particularly careful about going on these pills. Women who are practising the rhythm method, also known as 'natural family planning' or the safe period method, should also think twice before taking these pills. Where there is risk of pregnancy, taking tranquillisers or sleeping pills adds the further possible risk of birth defects.

On the whole it is best not to take these pills at any stage during pregnancy — except in medical emergencies. In the last three months of pregnancy, the pills become dangerous again. The unborn child can be born a tranquilliser addict if his or her mother is on these pills.

Some doctors have described what can only be called withdrawal symptoms in newborn babies whose mothers have been taking tranquillisers. More common is the so-called 'floppy infant syndrome'. The babies are floppy, sleepy, reluctant to suck, and may need special care. The higher the dose of the drug, the more severely affected the baby. 'Floppy infant syndrome' has been seen in babies whose mothers were on long-term but low doses of tranquillisers or sleeping pills.

Just as tranquillisers find their way through the body of a pregnant mother into the baby's body, so these drugs pass into the mother's milk. All babies do best if they can be breastfed for at least a few weeks after birth. But the mother who is taking either tranquillisers or sleeping pills while she nurses is passing these drugs on to her baby.

The only safe way then to avoid all these risks is *never* to take these pills just before, during or just after pregnancy. What is horrifying, however, are reports of these pills being given out in some antenatal wards.

Pills affect people differently

Nobody quite knows why, but some people react rather oddly to tranquillisers, showing what is called a 'paradoxical rage reaction'. They become aggressive, irritable and angry instead of tranquil and calm.

Here is a doctor's description of what happened to one woman who was given tranquillisers: 'She expressed a great deal of anger at her husband, her therapist, and her four-year-old daughter. She also began to act self-destructively. On once occasion, she banged her head repeatedly against the wall.'

People who react like this to tranquillisers are exceptions to the general rule that tranquillisers calm people down.

Some baby-battering cases seem to be triggered off when either the mother or the father starts taking tranquillisers. It may be that the pills remove their inhibitions and their previously pent-up anger comes out in action.

Most women will not experience this side-effect. But it is worth mentioning for those individuals who do. If you feel irritable, quarrelsome and angry after taking either tranquillisers or sleeping pills, go back to your doctor and tell him what the pills are doing to you. What is needed is not higher doses of the drug, but either a different drug or no drugs at all.

Tranquillisers, sleeping pills and alcohol

As the twelve-point safety plan for taking these pills makes clear, only a very small amount of alcohol indeed should *ever* be taken while you are on these pills. It is best not to drink at all.

The absolute limit, *with no exceptions*, is a single measure of spirits, a small glass of wine or a half pint of lager or beer. Better still, drink soft drinks if you are at a party or in the pub.

The reason for this is that tranquillisers, *and* sleeping pills, react with the alcohol to make its effects more powerful. A woman who takes tranquillisers and then drinks one pint of lager will be as drunk as a woman who has had several pints.

Sleeping pills, especially the long-acting ones, have the same effect as tranquillisers when it comes to drinking. Even though it is the evening after the night before, and the sleeping pill may have been taken almost twenty hours ago, its effect may still be in the body. If you take sleeping pills intermittently – probably the best way to make them — wait twenty-four hours after taking the pill before you drink more than the safe limit.

The dangers of mixing alcohol with these pills can be seen if we look at what effects the pills have. About 15 mg of diazepam (Valium) is something like the equivalent of a quarter bottle of whisky. If you are taking that during the day, more alcohol on top of it is going to make you drunk fairly fast.

When alcohol and these pills are taken together, you will

33

probably feel drunk more quickly, and your judgement will be impaired. If you are going to drive, do not drink *at all* — not even the one small drink permitted in the twelve-point plan.

Tranquillisers and other drugs

Tranquillisers do not mix well with other drugs which affect the central nervous system. Pills that are 'downers', like antihistamines for instance, should not be taken at the same time as tranquillisers. Do not take travel sickness pills if you are on tranquillisers or sleeping pills.

One or two other medical drugs have side-effects when combined with tranquillisers or sleeping pills. Tagamet, a common drug given for ulcers and hiatus hernia, stops the benzodiazepine drugs being passed out of the body, so their level builds up. Occasionally doctors forget this and prescribe Tagamet for ulcers, and tranquillisers for the stress which may have helped produce the ulcers. This is not a good idea.

Most doctors are aware of this, of course, since it is mentioned in the guideline fact sheets put out by the drug companies. But do not be afraid to question your doctor, if he prescribes a drug while you are already on tranquillisers or sleeping pills. You will be helping him by reminding him of this fact.

Most people forget that coffee, tea and tobacco are also drugs. All are stimulants — 'uppers' rather than 'downers'. Thus, if you drink endless cups of tea or coffee or smoke many cigarettes you will counter the 'downer' calming effect of the pills. Some soft drinks also contain caffeine and have a similar effect.

If, therefore, you find that your tranquillisers or sleeping pills don't seem to be working well enough, cut out coffee, tea and cigarettes. Do this *before* asking for a higher dosage — you may find you do not need one.

Occasionally women who have just started taking these pills find that they are drinking much more coffee or tea. Without consciously knowing it, they are trying to counter the sedating effects of the pill. If you find you are doing this, ask your doctor for a lower dose.

Tranquillisers and the elderly

Unfortunately, the statistics show that tranquillisers are more likely to be handed out to older than younger women. Yet there are special dangers in these pills for the old and the very elderly.

As the body grows older it is in general more powerfully affected by any kind of drug. A dose of tranquillisers which would be quite safe with a younger woman, may be dangerous to an elderly one. Because her body cannot rid itself of the drug, high levels of it build up.

It has been estimated that at least ten to fifteen per cent of women and men admitted to hospital geriatric wards are there because of illness produced by drugs. A consultant geriatrician said:

> You can improve twenty-five per cent of the patients coming in here dramatically by taking them off the tablets they are on. Digoxin, Largactil, Sparine, the tranquillisers and all sorts of drugs. Mogadon is a problem, they [GPs] don't think it is as troublesome as it is, but patients get confused because it lasts longer than it should. We take them off and they get better.

The other danger from tranquillisers and sleeping pills among the elderly is that they may be on so many other drugs at the same time. If they have a doctor who prescribes easily and gives repeat prescriptions they may be on a positive cocktail of drugs and medicines.

Some doctors take the view that the elderly should not take tranquillisers or sleeping pills at all. Certainly, old people who suffer from sleep apnoea (episodes during slumber of not breathing) should not be on sleeping pills, as pills may make the non-breathing worse.

Some drug manufacturers recommend specially small doses for the elderly. Others do not specify. But in general women and men over sixty years of age should be on half doses of tranquillisers and sleeping pills; over the age of eighty they should not be taking any tranquillisers or sleeping pills.

Long-term use of tranquillisers

There may be long-term risks in taking these drugs which

we do not yet know about. So far there has neither been the time nor the opportunity for enough medical research.

Those who are taking tranquillisers or sleeping pills for month after month face one danger we do know about — drug dependency. This side-effect of the benzodiazepine drugs may turn out to be one of the greatest risks of all.

FOUR

Becoming Dependent on Pills

Most people have strong ideas about drug addicts. They think of them as men and women who use drugs for kicks, and who use mainly illegal drugs. The image of a drug addict is a young person out of his mind with pot smoking, a hippie type using a needle to inject heroin, or a violent youngster sniffing glue for kicks. Our vision of drug addiction is nearly always that of street addiction — outcasts in the gutter because of their addiction.

Yet thousands of perfectly respectable women and men are now dependent upon drugs. If you meet them in the street you would not think: 'There goes a drug addict'. They look like ordinary people. They behave like ordinary people most of the time. They do not need needles or plastic bags for glue sniffing. Indeed they would be horrified by the idea. Many of them do not even know that they are addicted.

These are the addicts who have become dependent upon prescribed drugs — drugs which they get quite legally from their doctors. They probably started taking them for a very good medical reason, but they have continued to take them well after that reason no longer applied. Even their doctors may not always know that these addicts *are* dependent on their drugs.

Drug addiction is rather a mystery, even to the experts. Nowadays doctors tend to talk about 'drug dependence' — a phrase which sounds a little less frightening than addiction. The medical profession still fiercely disagrees on many of the hows and whys of drug dependence.

What is clear is that some drugs are much more addictive than others. Hard drugs like heroin and morphine carry a greater risk of dependence than soft drugs like cannabis. Even quite legally prescribed drugs can make people dependent. The barbiturates were known to cause drug dependence — that is one reason why doctors prescribe them only occasionally nowadays. As mentioned above, even a drug like aspirin may cause a few people to become addicted, and coffee certainly produces some caffeine addicts.

Dependence on tranquillisers

Nobody yet is quite sure exactly how addictive tranquillisers and sleeping pills are. But it is known that high doses are more likely to create dependence than low doses. The length of time you are taking the drug also makes a difference.

A person taking a high dose of these drugs may become dependent on them in a relatively short time. An abnormally high dose might make them dependent in two or three weeks. But a low dose might still make a person dependent if it was taken not just for months but for years.

One very perplexing fact is that some individuals seem to be more prone to drug dependence than others. Just as millions of people drink alcohol, but only a small proportion become alcoholics, so millions take pills but only a proportion become dependent on them. Some lucky individuals seem slower to succumb to drug dependence. Others may become hooked relatively easily.

Becoming dependent on a drug is not a sign of character weakness, psychological maladjustment or moral depravity. Some great women and men have become dependent on drugs — so have lots of ordinary people. Unfortunately nobody knows in advance *which* individuals are going to succumb to drug dependence — or why.

Doctors used to think that tranquillisers and sleeping pills of the benzodiazepine family were unlikely to be addictive in normal doses. Some took the view that even if they were addictive it did not really matter since the drugs were harmless. One theory was that the only people who were likely to become dependent on their drugs would be those who had a history of drug abuse or dependence — alcoholics or recovered alcoholics, heroin addicts and the like.

Medical opinion is slowly beginning to change. These drugs have now been in use long enough for some individuals to have been taking them for a very long time. Medical researchers, like Professor Malcolm Lader, are beginning to observe a set pattern of withdrawal symptoms when long-term tranquilliser takers stop taking their drug. If there is a withdrawal syndrome with these drugs, then clearly the drugs make people dependent on them.

Drug dependence is an illness, not a vice

Today doctors and scientists treat drug dependence as an illness. Like catching measles or getting pneumonia it is a misfortune, not a vice. People are not ashamed of catching influenza, so they should not be ashamed of 'catching' drug dependence.

But because some drug addicts — mainly young people taking hard drugs — behave badly, many people confuse drug dependence with immorality or vice. They do not understand clearly that people do not *choose* to become drug dependent; it is something that can happen against their will, and tranquillisers and sleeping pills are not illegal drugs.

Most women and men who have become dependent on tranquillisers or sleeping pills do not behave particularly badly because of their dependence. Inside the home, their behaviour may be noticeably slightly odd, but outside the home they usually seem perfectly normal to outsiders. Friends and relations will probably be completely unaware of their drug problem.

Nor should anybody be ashamed of having become dependent upon tranquillisers or sleeping pills. Nearly all dependent women were originally given these pills by their doctors in the first place. Often the doctor will have encouraged them to keep taking the tablets, saying that they are quite harmless. Patients believe, quite naturally, that the pills are doing them good.

But drug dependence, however it has occurred, should be tackled. If you have had the misfortune to become dependent upon your pills, you should try to get well. You, and only you, have to take the decision to tackle the problem. Nobody, however close the relationship, can do it for you.

Drug dependence — a problem of body and mind

Part of the mystery of drug dependence is that it affects the whole human being. Illnesses like measles affect mainly the body; illnesses like schizophrenia affect mainly the mind. Drug dependence affects both. And those who believe that human beings have a soul or a spirit often believe that drug dependence affects the spiritual side of a person's life too.

Doctors sometimes talk of drug dependence in two different ways: 'physical dependence' — the way the body has come to depend on the drug; and 'psychological dependence' — the way the person's mind depends on the drug.

There may be individuals who are mainly physically affected, and others who are mainly psychologically affected. But most people probably experience both physical and psychological dependence at the same time.

Physical dependence — how the body reacts
When a drug is used regularly, the body generally becomes used to it. People who take tranquillisers and sleeping pills feel the effects most strongly in the first two weeks of taking them. That is why they should not drive during this time. But after a couple of weeks the body probably learns to live with the drug. In fact, sometimes the body gets so used to the drug that it ceases to have much effect. Doctors call this developing 'tolerance' to a drug, which means that in order to get the same effect, one must start taking higher doses.

Becoming tolerant to a drug's effects is one sign that a drug is causing physical dependence. Anna's story in the next chapters (pages 54–5 and 61–3) shows how her pills no longer seemed to deal with her anxiety so she was given higher doses. But with tranquillisers and sleeping pills this does not always happen, even with people who are dependent.

Tranquilliser addicts sometimes do not become tolerant to the drug, and therefore do not go on to higher and higher doses. This is one reason why doctors were slow to recognize that tranquillisers and sleeping pills made people dependent.

People who take tranquillisers often have withdrawal symptoms when they stop taking their drugs. Everybody has heard what happens when a heroin addict goes 'cold turkey', or when an alcoholic has delirium tremens — these are withdrawal symptoms from heroin and alcohol respectively. Yet until recently very few people had heard of withdrawal symptoms from the benzodiazepine drugs.

These withdrawal symptoms are described more fully below in Chapter 7. But it is important to realize here that they only occur *when the addict has reduced her dose or stopped taking the drug*. Women who continue to take their pills will never have experienced them, though they could be addicts without even knowing it.

For many people the first signs of drug dependence may be these withdrawal symptoms when the drug is stopped, or when the dose is reduced. Sometimes women get the symptoms if they have forgotten to take their pills at the right time, or if they have left home without them.

Psychological dependence — how the mind reacts
Psychological dependence is rather more difficult to explain than physical dependence. Basically a woman who is psychologically dependent upon a drug begins to rely on the mood alteration that the drug produces, as it either makes her feel good or at least stops her feeling bad.

The psychologically dependent woman may have got into the habit of using the drug to deal with her emotions. If she is anxious she takes a pill. If she is edgy she takes a pill. If she gets a fright she takes a pill.

Another sign of psychological dependence is that the addict starts making extra sure she has supplies of her drug. She may try to get extra prescriptions — to use in case she loses pills. Getting and taking the drug becomes increasingly important in her life. At the end of her addiction, Anna started doing this (page 54).

The psychological side of dependence is important. It is one reason why addicts so often go back to their drugs, even when they have been weaned off them. Somebody who has been using tranquillisers or sleeping pills to blot out their emotions or deal with difficulties in life, may find life without a pill extremely difficult, at least to begin with.

Uncomfortable feelings like anger, anxiety or pain seem extraordinarily intense. Ordinary people learn to live with or deal with these feelings as they come. But an addict may have spent years blotting them out with a pill. She may crave the escape that the pill used to give her.

Thus, even when the bodily withdrawal symptoms have died away, a woman who was dependent upon drugs may still be left with a craving for some kind of pill. The psychological side of dependence may continue. An addict has to stop taking her drug; she also has to learn how to stay off it.

The vicious circle

Drug dependence is a vicious circle. Its symptoms can be very confusing indeed. The dependent person feels she *needs* the drug to keep going, but this feeling of need may be a sign of dependence. It is often difficult for the addict herself to know what is going on.

Both tranquillisers and sleeping pills have a short rebound effect, after they have been taken for only small periods of time. After stopping tranquillisers, there will be two or three days of anxiety. In addition to this there is the withdrawal effect which happens after a woman has become dependent on her pills. This withdrawal effect includes sometimes severe anxiety, feeling ill, and insomnia, new symptoms which do not occur in the ordinary rebound effect.

The result is a vicious circle. If, for instance, a woman has taken tranquillisers for several months then decides she will stop the pills — the first thing that happens is that she feels anxious, either just a few days of rebound anxiety or perhaps weeks of severe withdrawal anxiety.

Because she does not understand about the rebound and withdrawal effects, she thinks that this is the original anxiety for which the pills were prescribed coming back. Naturally she concludes that she still needs her pills. She goes back on tranquillisers — thus increasing the risk of becoming dependent, if she is not already so.

Sleeping pills have much the same effect. After only a few days on sleeping pills, there is a rebound effect of insomnia. A woman who has been taking nightly pills for even just a few days, will probably find that when she stops taking them she suffers from insomnia.

This is 'sleeping pill insomnia', caused by the rebound effect of the pills. But the patient does not know this. She just thinks that it is her original insomnia coming back. What does she do? She concludes that she still needs the pills, so she starts taking them again.

Occasionally the short-acting sleeping pills may have a rebound effect the following day. Tests with triazolam (Halcion) show that women who take it at night may suffer from anxiety later the following day — in other words, rebound anxiety.

Unfortunately women do not realize this. They may begin to wonder if they need tranquillisers during the day to deal with the anxiety. Once again a vicious circle of pill-taking has been set up.

Facing the truth

It is extremely painful for any woman to face the truth — that she may be dependent upon her tranquillisers or sleeping pills. Nobody *wants* to admit to being drug dependent. Wishful thinking or rationalizing will try to persuade most people that perhaps they are not.

Many women make excuses for their pills: 'I'd never be able to sleep without them'; 'I just couldn't face life without them'; 'I *need* these pills'; 'When I don't have them, I simply can't cope.' Excuses like these sometimes show just how strongly a person is dependent on the drug.

Some excuses are more subtle: 'I know some women are dependent on these pills but I am different because . . .'; 'I could stop taking them any time but just now I have got to go on taking them because . . .'; 'My husband says he cannot live with me unless I keep taking my pills . . . .'

Sometimes doctors help by giving reasons for continuing on the pills: 'My doctor says that they are not harming me'; 'I asked my doctor and he said I should go on taking them.' Sometimes the doctor really did say this; sometimes it is not quite what he or she said, but the woman refuses to remember the exact words.

Such excuses are the natural result of not wanting to face the truth. Yet, if a woman is going to recover from drug dependence she needs, above all, to be honest with herself. Only by facing up to her problem can she begin to conquer it. Excuses just help her stay ill, when she needs to begin to get well.

How bad is the problem?

There is enormous disagreement among the experts about the number of people who are dependent on tranquillisers or sleeping pills. In 1980 one medical expert suggested that there was only one case of tranquilliser addiction for every five to ten million months of use by patients. If doses were always kept within the safe limits then the risk was only one in every fifty million months of patient use.

This is beginning to seem like a wildly optimistic calculation, now that more attention is being paid to the problem of tranquilliser dependence. Many years ago the experts believed that the barbiturates were not at all addictive. It was only as time passed and more cases of addiction arose that they had to change their minds.

Professor Malcolm Lader, of the Institute of Psychiatry, estimates that the number of people in Britain who have become dependent on their drugs is probably between 100 000 to 250 000. 'In terms of numbers the problem is five times that of heroin.'

Certainly the addiction problem of tranquillisers has probably been underestimated in the past. Many more women than expected are anxious about their tranquilliser use. In 1982 a London radio station, LBC, ran seven hours of programmes about drugs, alcohol and even addiction to food during one week. Only one out of ten programmes was specifically about prescribed drugs, and five of the programmes were specifically *not* about them.

Yet the phone calls which came in from listeners were mainly about tranquillisers. 'Tranquillisers constituted the most common concern, 899, or sixty-one per cent of all the calls,' said a report of the radio project. 'The number of years some callers had been taking such drugs warrants discussion in the medical world, as does the reason why some of these callers had been prescribed drugs in the first place.'

Indeed the radio programme organizers had not been expecting so many calls on this topic. 'The years of tranquilliser consumption were staggering, from six months to thirty years. Many callers were elderly women, sixty, seventy and seventy-five years old, now unable to cope with a day if they did not take their drugs. . . .Slowly the counselling team realized that what was being discussed was addiction.'

One reason why doctors may have underestimated the problem emerged during the radio programmes. Many telephone callers said that they felt they could not talk to their doctors. One thirty-seven-year-old woman called to say: 'I've just seen a programme about tranquillisers. Do tranquillisers make your brain soft? Because I've been taking them for fifteen years and I can't stop.' She went on, 'If I stop, I can't get through the day. My doctor won't listen, he just says I need calming down and writes me another prescription. No-one will help me.'

Similar cries for help have been reported by MIND, the National Association for Mental Health in Britain, which runs an advice service. In 1981 this advice service reported:

> Many people take these drugs daily, but it is not known to what extent the therapeutic course of treatment has been exceeded. As far as the advice service can judge from requests for help, this number is considerable and alarming, and dependence on benzodiazepines, whether or not psychological, is a growing problem.

Knowing whether you are dependent

If any of the following six statements applies to you, then you may have become dependent upon tranquillisers.

1. You have been taking tranquillisers or sleeping pills for six months or more continuously.

2. You are taking more than the normal prescribed dose, or more than the dose prescribed for severe anxiety or insomnia. Consult the dosage chart on page 25.

3. You have asked your doctor to increase the dose; you are taking larger doses than instructed, or taking the same dose more often than instructed; you are getting extra pills from elsewhere; you always make sure you have an adequate supply of drugs.

4. You are mixing your drugs with alcohol, or with other drugs such as antihistamines. (If in doubt about this

question, ask your doctor again *exactly* what other drugs you can take.)

5. The drug is interfering with your life in some way, causing difficulties in family relationships or social life or work or housework or any other activity.

6. You get withdrawal symptoms when you do not take your normal dose. These symptoms include feeling ill (like a bout of influenza), being jumpy, irritable, sleepless, aching muscles and pains, sensitivity to lights and sounds, feeling unsteady or seasick, sweating, palpitations, nausea, and anxiety.

If any of these six danger signs applies to you, you should think about coming off the drug. But *do nothing* about it, until you have read Chapter 7 on how to come off.

Because most women don't want to think of themselves as drug dependent, they may be tempted to give these statements just a brief look. It is worth examining them more carefully.

1. *You have been taking sleeping pills or tranquillisers continuously for six months or more.*

There are some rare individuals who have to take these pills for longer than six months for good medical reasons. But on the whole, after six months these pills are not doing you any good. The longer you are on them, the greater the risk of dependence.

2. *You have been taking more than the normal prescribed dose, or more than the higher dose prescribed for severe anxiety or insomnia.*

You will need to consult the dosage chart (page 25), to work out whether your daily intake of drugs is higher than the normal daily dose. The particular daily limit varies according to the kind of drug you take. On pages 9–10 is a list of all the drugs, with their British brand names.

If you are taking both tranquillisers *and* sleeping pills, then the combination of both pills may mean you are over the recommended limit. For instance, if you are taking lorazepam (Ativan), the daily total limit is 10 mg. Sleeping pills on top of this puts you above the limit.

The converse is also true. For example, the recommended dose of flunitrazepam (Rohypnol) for severe insomnia is up to 2 mg. If you are taking tranquillisers on top of this, you are exceeding the recommended limit.

3. *You have asked your doctor to increase the dose; you are taking larger doses than instructed or the same dose more often; you are getting extra pills from elsewhere: you always make sure you have an adequate supply of drugs.*

Be honest in considering this. Have you ever increased the dose to get over a bad moment? Have you found yourself taking the pills half an hour earlier than you should? Do you feel tense waiting for the right time for the pills? Have you got a spare prescription tucked away somewhere just in case you lose your current one? Do you feel that you *need* a higher dose?

With some people on these pills, the dose seems to creep slowly upwards. Perhaps they are not exactly asking the doctor for more, but nevertheless they present themselves in such a way that he prescribes more. If your dose is slowly creeping upwards, this may be a sign that you are developing a tolerance to the drug and possibly drug dependence.

4. *You are mixing your drugs with alcohol or other drugs*

Be honest about the alcohol. Do you drink more than one small sherry, a measure of spirits, or half a pint of beer a day? Have you *ever* drunk more? Do you feel that this limit somehow does not apply to you?

Do you include sleeping pills in this? Taking sleeping pills and drinking is just the same as taking tranquillisers and drinking. Do you take antihistamines with your pills? What about cough mixtures, or those night preparations for colds? Do you smoke pot? Do you take any illegal drugs?

If you are in doubt, write down a weekly diary of exactly when you take your pills, what kind they are, and exactly how much you drink. Count in any cough mixtures or painkillers.

5. *The drug is interfering with your life in some way, causing difficulties in family relationships, social life, work, housework or any other activity.*

Have any members of the family complained about your behaviour recently, or asked you about the pills. Are you unnecessarily irritable, forgetful, vague, unable to cope? Have you dropped hobbies or interests you used to have?

Do you find housework particularly difficult? Are there complaints about your work? Do you feel unable to go out to parties? Do you not enjoy outside entertainments? Is your marriage showing signs of stress?

6. *You get withdrawal symptoms when you do not take your normal dose.*

Some people never get these symptoms because they never stop their pills. If you keep on taking the pills, you will simply not know if you become dependent.

But if you have ever forgotten a pill, or forgotten to renew the prescription in time, or been caught outside the home without the pills, you may have experienced symptoms of withdrawal, which some people do not recognize; they think they have caught influenza, or even that they are having a nervous breakdown.

If you have had this kind of experience, think back. Was it when you stopped taking the pills? Did you feel better when you started taking them again?

If you have had to agree with one or more of the above statements, then you are at risk of having become dependent on these drugs. Do not be dismayed or disheartened. There are now hundred of women who have managed to conquer their addiction. Six examples follow in Chapters 5 and 6.

FIVE

Six Case Histories

Most women who take tranquillisers or sleeping pills do so on their doctor's orders. They are conscientious about taking the right dose, and they would be horrified to think of themselves as potential drug addicts. Yet there are now thousands of women who are at great risk of becoming addicted to their pills.

Though there is no proof that these pills help anxiety after four month's use, nevertheless there are thousands of women and men who have been taking these pills for longer periods. One in forty people, according to the surveys, will have taken these drugs daily for at least a year — eight months longer than recommended by the Committee on the Review of Medicine.

Thanks to the earlier conviction that these were safe pills there are now thousands of people who have been on tranquillisers or sleeping pills as a matter of daily routine not just for months, but for years. Some of them have by now been taking the pills for as long as twenty years. These people are at the greatest risk of drifting into drug dependence.

Drug abuse and drug dependence

Drug abuse is not the same as drug dependence. Drug abuse occurs when individuals misuse drugs. A woman who abuses tranquillisers will take more than are prescribed, mix her pills with alcohol or other drugs, or take the pills not for anxiety but just for kicks.

The benzodiazepine drugs are rarely abused. Women who take them just for kicks are few and far between. When abuse does occur, it is usually by women who are already either alcoholics or addicted to other drugs. 'Twenty per cent of the residents coming through here are abusing Valium to quite a heavy degree,' reported the City Road

Drug Project, a centre for treating hard drug addicts in London, in 1981.

However, drug abuse does not always coincide with drug dependence. It is quite possible to become dependent on these pills *without ever abusing them*. Women who follow their doctor's orders, and who *never* take more than ordered, can nevertheless end up dependent on the drug.

Drug dependence is the modern word for drug addiction. People who are dependent on their drugs take them as a habit, they come to rely on the drug, and when they stop taking it they suffer withdrawal symptoms. Sometimes people who have already become dependent on their drugs begin to abuse them as well.

It is only too easy for perfectly respectable, sensible women to drift into drug dependence. Tranquillisers and sleeping pills are sometimes taken for years on doctor's orders. In this way otherwise responsible and careful women find that they have become dependent on these drugs.

Jane — pills without problems
Jane is thirty-six, married with three children and a husband who is a business executive. Four years ago she had her last child, and found herself very upset after the birth. She says:

> He was rather a fretful baby and I think that's what may have set off the baby blues. As well as that, we'd just come back from abroad and my husband was changing jobs. It was a difficult time....I lost an awful lot of weight. I just couldn't eat. My parents were shocked when they saw me. I was terrible. My doctor prescribed antidepressants and tranquillisers for me....From feeling ghastly, within a week I felt much better. He gave me a repeat prescription and I went on taking them. I stopped the antidepressants after a few months and just stayed on Librium. I took a pill three times a day.

Sometime in the following year, Jane read a newspaper article about tranquillisers which really frightened her: 'I thought I must stop taking them. Here's my chance to do so while I'm still frightened.'

For Jane the decision was simple — so were the results. Though she had been taking the pills for more than a year she was not addicted to them. She stopped without difficulty.

Margaret — the housewife who followed doctor's orders
Margaret is fifty-six. She has been a mother and a housewife most of her life. She started taking tranquillisers about twenty years ago. 'I wasn't sleeping very well and I was nervous and jumpy. The doctor gave me Nembutal, a barbiturate sleeping pill.'

He also prescribed Librium, which made her very depressed. So he changed the pills to Valium, and Margaret settled down to a daily dose of 20 mg, which is within the safe limit.

'I never increased the dose — not even if I knew something was coming up that would make me very nervous. I'd still stick to the right dose.'

About four or five years ago, she went back to her doctor and asked him, 'Haven't I been on these tablets long enough?' 'Don't worry. I'll give you something else which is much better for you,' said her doctor. He handed out a prescription for diazepam — exactly the same formula as Valium, but a different name. Because Margaret was not an expert on drugs, she did not know that the doctor had simply deceived her into thinking this was a different drug.

Two years later she had to go into hospital for a thyroid operation. The doctor there told her that she shouldn't still be taking the tranquillisers. 'When I went back to my family doctor and told him, he just said: "Stuff the hospital. They're not doing you any harm."'

But they were. Margaret was beginning to feel increasingly unable to cope.

I thought perhaps I was getting prematurely senile. I had nursed my mother when she was old and senile and I felt I was getting just like her....There were no ups and downs in my life. I had no pleasure in anything. When I saw someone coming to the door I wanted to hide....I couldn't remember how to cook. I've always been the sort of cook who doesn't have to measure things. Now I couldn't even make custard. It was either too thick or too thin. I blamed the milk, or I blamed the custard powder. But it was me....My eyes seemed to go peculiar too. I am very fond of needlework, but I had to stop doing it. I just couldn't do it.... I just kept on taking the pills because I thought they must be doing me good. Yet my mind was so muddled that I had to write everything down, if I wanted to remember it.

Without knowing it, over the years Margaret had become dependent on the pills.

Beth — a lifetime's insomnia
Beth is seventy years old, with children and grandchildren. Apart from a touch of arthritis she is well, and spends much of her time painting oil pictures, which she shows in good London exhibitions.

During a not very successful marriage to an estate agent, she brought up two children. All her life she has been an insomniac, and in 1956 when her youngest child was twelve she was first prescribed barbiturate sleeping pills, Sodium Amytal. She took them for a few months, then stopped without difficulty.

In the winter of that year her sister was diagnosed as having lung cancer and went into hospital to die. Beth was very upset. Her doctor prescribed Seconal as a daytime sedative and more Sodium Amytal for sleep, both barbiturates.

After six months of these Beth felt she was becoming addicted. Very slowly she managed to stop taking the Seconal, then over a whole year and a half she got off the Sodium Amytal. 'It took a long time. I weaned myself off by reducing the dose very, very slowly.'

Her marriage, which had never been good, broke up in 1961. Devastated by the impending divorce, she again turned to the doctor for help and was given yet another barbiturate sleeping pill, Soneryl. After two years on these pills, Beth began to feel she was addicted again. Once again, she wearily weaned herself off them.

In 1969 a new doctor gave her Mogadon, one of the benzodiazepine sleeping pills. He assured her that they were harmless, and that it would not matter this time if she did become dependent on them. They would not affect her in any way.

'I took them for the next eight years. I never exceeded the dose. The doctor said I could have one or two a night. I never took more than about one and a half. By this time, I was wary of all pills.'

But in 1977 she began to wonder if perhaps even these new, harmless pills were doing her good:

It was lovely to get a good night's rest from them, but I began to feel they were destroying my brain. I was forgetful, unable to concentrate and very vague....It's rather difficult to describe what was happening. But I was not able to get my brain together to do something important. I would be fizzing with alertness about it, but somehow I couldn't apply myself to it.

Perhaps because she had previously been dependent on the barbiturate pills, Beth began to wonder whether these sleeping pills were quite as harmless as the doctor had said. She could recognize that she had become dependent on them — just as she had been dependent on the earlier barbiturates.

Joan — she started helping others
Joan is a strong-minded woman in her forties who runs a self-help group for women and men who want to get off tranquillisers. She is energetic in her attempts to help others in the problem she faced herself.

She started taking tranquillisers in 1963. 'My ex-husband was battering me. I went to the doctor and she gave me some tranquillisers. That didn't stop my ex-husband hitting me, but the pills subdued me so that I let him do it.'

For the next seventeen years she duly collected her prescriptions from her doctor. 'On many occasions I asked why I was so irritable and aggressive. Could it be the pills? But my woman doctor told me they were more or less sweeties and many people took more than I did.'

She also collected other pills on and off. 'One thing leads to another. Tranquillisers make you depressed so I got antidepressants. I also got Mogadon sleeping pills and barbiturates. I never asked for these pills, but the doctor said I needed them.'

The last few years of Joan's pill-taking are not very clear in her memory, but she does not think she ever abused the pills. She just took the 15 mg a day that the doctor ordered. 'My doctor said take them, so I did.'

The only exception to this was that she noticed that she wanted the pills sooner: 'I'd find I was wanting to take one an hour earlier than I should'.

One day when she was sitting in her office, she decided

she was going to try and get off her tranquillisers: 'I'll do it myself,' she thought. She started reducing the dose.

Her immediate reaction was to feel violently giddy and sick. She went to her doctor and told her what she was doing. 'You want more pills not less,' said the doctor. Joan went back on her pills obediently. But she still felt she ought to stop them eventually.

Anna — *dependence led to abuse*

Anna is a well-dressed woman in her forties with a job in management consultancy, who certainly does not look like the kind of person who becomes an addict. But nevertheless Anna became addicted to tranquillisers.

She first took the pills at the age of twenty-six. She had gone to the USA to take a job in advertising, which at first went well. But after a few months she started getting panic attacks. 'I had ulcer symptoms. I was depressed, and I was frightened.'

For eighteen months she had regular appointments with a woman psychiatrist who prescribed Librium and anti-depressants. Anna feels that the pills helped her during this period. When the psychiatrist left the country, she left Anna a repeat prescription for the Librium.

Five years later Anna returned to England where she started a new career in management consultancy. 'I went back to college first, and then started climbing the ladder all over again. It's still a man's world and I had to work hard.'

By this time she was on a small but regular dose of Librium. 'But I began to feel funny. It's exactly the same feeling as you had when you went to the doctor in the first place. You say to yourself "It must be my nerves."'

Her new English doctor changed her from Librium to Valium. By this time the dose had increased and she was taking 15 mg four times a day — at his instructions. But this daily dose of 60 mg was *twice* the normal limit.

Nor did it seem to calm her down. 'I had terrible attacks of panic. I also got bouts of deep depression. I felt my memory was beginning to go. My legs went wobbly and I felt sick.'

On five occasions she went into the casualty department of hospitals, and she visited her doctor complaining of these symptoms numerous times. 'Every time I complained, I was told it was probably the change of life. I was given a drug for that, and also tried on two different sorts of tranquillisers. But nobody suggested stopping the tranquillisers.'

She began to be a permanent fixture in the doctor's surgery. By now she was taking all kinds of drugs, many of them prescribed by the doctor, to deal with the side-effects of the tranquillisers. At this point she began to abuse her drugs.

She started taking an extra pill if she felt particularly bad — or taking her dose a little earlier than normal. 'I was becoming so physically ill that I thought I was going mad. I had begun to line up two or three doctors, so that I could get more prescriptions.'

There were pills all over her flat. 'I was doing all the things that an addict does. I was making sure I had my supply. Yet it was all terribly socially acceptable, unlike being a heroin addict. I was hooked. Very slowly I began to realize it.'

Elaine — *first drug addiction then alcohol*

Elaine is in her seventies, a grey-haired energetic woman who buzzes round London in her Mini seeing friends and helping others who share her problem. Nowadays she laughs when she tells her story, even though it is a very sad one.

From the very start Elaine's life was mixed up with pills, and to a lesser extent alcohol. At the age of seventeen, when she started going to parties, she discovered that a few drinks made her feel less nervous. And when she got back home after such occasions she discovered she could not sleep. So she started buying sleeping pills from the chemist — this was perfectly legal before the last war.

When she married at the age of twenty-nine she became a total insomniac. A friend gave her a prescription, which she used to get bromide and chloral. 'It was wonderful. After I'd taken it I'd just fall back on the bed knocked out.'

At the age of forty-five she had a nervous breakdown when she discovered her husband was unfaithful. She spent three weeks in a nursing home and was put on barbiturates by the psychiatrist. 'I was also given sleeping pills. I'm not sure what kind. I would take two, and then if I couldn't sleep I would take two more, and then a further two. Somewhere over the next ten years my sedatives were changed to Librium.'

The nursing home also suggested that a regular bottle of stout would 'build her up'. She followed their advice and drank a bottle a night — at first.

Then at the age of sixty she finally left her husband. She began to get asthma attacks and was put on cortisone. She went back into the nursing home 'because of my nerves', and had to be transferred to a chest hospital because her breathing almost stopped altogether.

At this point the hospital stopped her pills because they thought they were interfering with her breathing. 'I wanted to die. I saw all kinds of things. I lost my sense of balance and I couldn't swallow. Finally I begged the hospital to put me back into the nursing home, where I could find my regular psychiatrist.'

Back at the nursing home she was put back on to Librium. She felt better, went home, and started a life revolved round pills and drink. For the original nightly bottle of stout had slowly escalated to a single very stiff whisky. 'A whole glassful actually,' admits Elaine. 'It was a tumblerful of whisky.'

She never drank during the day. Daytime was for Librium pills. She always waited for six o'clock in the evening. 'I found it hard to wait. The weekends were the worst. I felt terribly lonely then. I'd sit and look at the bottle waiting for the time. It had become an obsession.'

Taken on its own, Elaine's drinking was not at all that heavy. She was not drinking either during the morning or the afternoon. Yet because she was taking tranquillisers as well, the alcohol effects were magnified. Elaine had become addicted to both alcohol and tranquillisers at the age of sixty-four.

SIX

How the Case Histories Got Better

Admitting to a drug problem is not easy. It is even more difficult to take the next step, which is doing something about it. Some women have a moment of truth about their problem, and swing straight into action. Others know that they have a problem a long time before they can get the courage to start dealing with it.

Women's experiences of withdrawing from tranquillisers and sleeping pills vary. In the same way the extent of their dependence upon pills varies. Some lucky women find that they can reduce their pills to nothing without any difficulty at all. They wonder what all the fuss is about.

Others find that stopping is unexpectedly difficult. At times their courage and confidence almost fails them, but somehow they manage to go on. Chapter 5 gave six case histories on dependence; the following is how these women faced, dealt with and finally conquered their dependence on tranquillisers and sleeping pills.

Overcoming dependence

Jane — pills without problems
When Jane decided to stop taking her Librium, she just stopped taking it overnight. Stopping abruptly is not a good idea, but she did not know that. She felt very positive about stopping.

'I had no problems at all — no insomnia, no anxiety, nothing. Since then I've heard that some people do have problems stopping their pills, but I didn't. I must have been taking them for well over a year but it didn't seem to matter.'

The only slight difficulty she had — and it *was* only a slight one — was breaking the habit of taking a pill. So instead of taking a tranquilliser she used to take a vitamin tablet instead. 'It was the highlight of the day,' she jokes.

Jane is glad that she was given the tranquillisers when she needed them. 'Without them I don't know how I should have coped. They certainly helped me over a difficult patch.'

Margaret — the housewife who followed doctor's orders
Margaret had felt several times that she wanted to stop taking her pills, but it was when she read an article about tranquilliser dependence that she made up her mind. 'It struck me straight away — this is *me*. I told my daughter immediately, and I rang up Tranx, the self-help group mentioned in the article.'

Margaret decided she would not go back and see her doctor. She had little faith in him ever since he had given her diazepam without telling her it was just the same drug as Valium. She felt she could not rely on him.

Instead, she went to meetings of Tranx. The first step for her was to stop taking her sleeping pills, which were barbiturates. She did not find that too hard. But cutting down on her tranquillisers was much more difficult.

'It was hard, but it worked. I felt noises very acutely, and lights very brightly. I couldn't stand having my grandchildren around at first.'

To her dismay, her hair began falling out while she was slowly coming off the pills, and her nails broke. She experienced a lot of withdrawal symptoms. But by going to the self-help group weekly, she was able to recognize these for what they were.

She also learned something which has stood her in good stead — that she can just live through bad feelings. They do not last for ever.

> If I get a panic attack and I start to shake, then I just shake. I know I could stop by taking a pill, but that's the last thing I want to do. I've learned that it doesn't *matter* if I shake....I also find it helps to help others. I am able to tell women who come to Tranx meetings 'I was like you'. And sometimes people tell me how much better I look now.

Margaret is not ashamed to tell people what happened to her. 'At first I wasn't going to tell my friends. Then I thought "Well, it's not my fault." They have been very understanding.'

She welcomes all the small signs that her life is becoming normal and healthy. She has taken up her needlework again — something which she always enjoyed but could not do while she was on tranquillisers. And nowadays she can make custard, for instance, without any of the difficulty she experienced when she was on pills.

Today she does not take any tranquillisers or any sleeping pills. She is even wary of taking a painkiller for arthritis. Looking back she says: 'I think I must have realized what was happening in one of my clear periods. Otherwise I'd still be on the pills, my mind had got so muddled.'

Beth — *a lifetime's insomnia*

When Beth began to realize that her sleeping pills were doing her harm, she knew what to do. Twice the past she had already weaned herself off barbiturates, by slowly reducing the dose. Now it was time for her to do the same with these new sleeping pills.

She did not go to the doctor for advice, for he was the one who had told her in the first place that the pills could not harm her. She did not even tell her family at first. Her children seemed too bound up in their own lives. When she did tell them, they did not really understand what a struggle it was.

She just started cutting down the dose — breaking up the tablets first into half, then into quarters, and finally into small crumbs.

> It took me several months and it was awfully hard work. My insomnia came back in raging form. I got palpitations, and I was terribly anxious much of the time....But when I had finally stopped taking any pills at all, my brain slowly and markedly got better. *Markedly* better. I was less forgetful and less vague. The pills had made me less able to cope with bad situations, even though the doctor had said they could not harm me.

Stopping taking the pills altogether and never taking another one has not been easy for her. 'I had a great urge to take a pill when I first stopped them, and I still get a longing for one occasionally. But I simply don't give in to it. My doctor has offered me them again, and I find it rather a strain refusing them. But I know I have got better since I stopped taking them.'

Beth is still an insomniac. Without the pills she finds it difficult to get to sleep. 'The worst thing is that you no longer know that you will sleep. When I was taking the pills, I knew that they would make me sleep.'

She struggles through the night.

Now I know that I might not sleep, and that makes me worry. If I'm feeling very tired, I think: 'Oh goodness, I may not get to sleep'. But I have got better about not worrying. I try to accept my insomnia now as just one of those things....A hot drink of milk and honey sometimes helps if I can't sleep. I also find that putting a hot water bottle or an electric heating pad on my tummy and cuddling it helps.

Part of her sleeping difficulties stem from arthritis, which makes her ache at night. She takes small doses of ordinary aspirin painkillers for that.

What pleases her most is that her oil painting has improved in skill and inspiration since she stopped her sleeping pills. 'The other day somebody said what better work I was doing. I feel that's thanks to stopping the pills.'

Joan — she started helping others

Joan's experience of coming off tranquillisers was a bad one. The first shock was when she went to her doctor's surgery and found a new young doctor there. 'Why are you on these things?' he said. 'I'm not going to give you any more.'

The next morning after this dangerously abrupt withdrawal of all the pills, Joan woke up suicidal. 'I was horrified. I managed somehow to get through the day and I went back to the doctor and told him how I felt. He wasn't helpful.'

In desperation she went to another doctor, got some pills, and went back on the tranquillisers. But after about a week she started reducing the dose. 'All this had shown me that I was an addict. I just couldn't do without the bloody things. So I started a very slow withdrawal over four months.'

Using a nail file, she started grinding down her pills into smaller and smaller sizes, until she had got down to little crumbs. 'I felt very grotty all this time, but I had no chance. It was survivable. I managed to get to work.'

When she had reduced her pills down to about 2 mg a day, she met a doctor who ran the alcoholic unit of a nearby hospital. He offered to admit her to a bed in his unit. She postponed the final coming off the pills until after Christmas by which time she was taking only a crumb of tranquillisers three times a day.

For six weeks her final withdrawal was supervised in hospital: 'I think if I'd done it at home with nobody to talk to, I'd have gone back on', she admits.

When she got out of hospital, Joan decided to do something to help others. She had been lucky to get into a special hospital unit — most women would not get the chance. She started up Tranx, a self-help group, which advises other women and men how to stop their pills.

'It was well worth the suffering of coming off. I now sleep nine hours a night. I don't feel depressed any more. I can think clearly, and I am my real self with my own emotions.'

She believes that she must never touch another tranquilliser or a sleeping pill. She is also a non-drinker.

> The danger is that, as an addict, I might switch my addiction from tranquillisers to alcohol. Not drinking is a precaution against this.... When you are coming off, it's important to realize that every minute that goes by is a minute nearer recovery. Every hour is an hour nearer recovery. Just concentrate on getting through the day.... For me it was worth everything to stop. I feel on top of the world now.

Anna — *dependence led to abuse*
Anna was in her early forties when she began to be severely ill from her tranquillisers. She had been taking them for almost twenty years by the end, and was on a dose which was double the normally accepted limit.

Not surprisingly, getting off the drug was difficult. She began to do something about her drug problem in 1980, when even less was known about tranquilliser dependence than now. She had no medical advice or support, but with courage and persistence she managed.

The first glimmer of truth came to her when she visited her normal doctor, only to find a locum in charge. 'You're taking far too many tranquillisers. I beg you to come off them,' he said, and he handed her out half her normal dose.

Anna's almost immediate reaction was to feel very ill. 'I was very cross and I felt dreadful. I quickly developed what my usual doctor diagnosed as mumps and pancreatitis. Now I wonder if it wasn't just withdrawals.'

Her normal dose of 60 mg was then restored. Then Anna met a woman called Jenny who had been both an alcoholic and an addict. Jenny went to Alcoholics Anonymous meetings to stay sober, and to a new organization called Narcotics Anonymous which helped her stay off drugs. She told Anna that she should go to Narcotics Anonymous.

By this time Anna had already begun to realize that she was hooked on her pills and that, far from doing her good, they were doing her harm. She went back to her doctor to ask if she could stop them. 'He just said, "Don't stop taking them. Don't come off." '

She decided to plan a programme of coming off. She started to cut down the amount, very slowly and very cautiously. She knew that she must taper off slowly, without help from any medical source. In all it took her two-and-a-half-years to come off.

She started feeling ill from the withdrawal symptoms, so she went to her doctor again.

> I asked him if there was something I could take to help me. He gave me Ativan. But by this time I'd bought a dictionary of drugs, so I looked it up before taking the pills. When I found out that it was just another tranquilliser I threw the pills away....By then I was going regularly to Narcotics Anonymous meetings. They were a great help. Being addicted to tranquillisers is a disease of isolation. You feel you are the only one with the problem. At NA I knew there were other people who had made it.

Her withdrawals were severe, because she had been on a high dose for so long. When she finally stopped the pills altogether, she had six weeks off work, in bed much of the time.

'It's the nature of the addiction that tells you that you are not getting better when you come off the drugs. But you are. You just *feel* worse. In the end I had been feeling so bad *on* tranquillisers, that I just had to get off them.'

At first Anna felt a violent anger against the medical profession. At Narcotics Anonymous meetings she talked about this and got it out in the open. 'Ninety-nine per cent of the difficulty of getting off the pills was fighting against my doctors. But I couldn't go on having negative feelings. I realized I had to change from anger to positive feelings.'

Anna feels that her long years of high tranquilliser doses may have left her with some brain damage.

> I notice it when I have to do concentrated thinking work. My span for concentration is only five hours. I do still get ringing in the ears, neuritis and physical pains too....I have had to throw away a lot of pills. There were piles of little pill bottles all over the house. Now I am extremely cautious about pills, even just an aspirin, and I don't drink alcohol at all.

From the outside Anna does not seem anything other than a well-organized and outgoing person. 'The most dramatic thing is how my brain function has improved. My eyesight is better. My memory is *far* better. And since I came off the pills completely I have never felt anxious or depressed.'

Elaine — first drug addiction then alcohol
Elaine began to realize something was wrong with her when she found the bathroom carpet sopping wet one morning. She called in the plumber and insisted there had been a leak. The plumber insisted there was *no* leak.

Slowly it began to dawn on Elaine that what had happened was that her bath had overflowed — but she had been too blotted out with tranquillisers and whisky to notice it. In a moment of truth she rang Alcoholics Anonymous.

After going to one of their meetings, she stopped drinking alcohol — but she still had to face the problem of her tranquilliser dependence. 'All in all, it took me seven weeks to get off the pills.'

Fortunately she had a helpful psychiatrist. He booked her into a nursing home, and started tapering off her pills. At the same time Elaine was going from the nursing home to two Alcoholic Anonymous meetings a day, where she felt there was encouragement and support for both her drink and drug problem.

> Eventually I just cut the pills right out. There followed ten days of utter hell. I remember I was hallucinating at 3.00 am in the morning, and I rang my AA sponsor. He just talked to me until I felt better....The other thing was fear. I think I felt fear almost all the time. But I was determined that I wouldn't take another mind-bending pill. So I kept close to AA.

Nine years later, Elaine feels it was all worthwhile. She still goes to Alcoholics Anonymous meetings, and occasionally to Narcotics Anonymous. She tries to help others in the way she herself was helped.

> I am still a natural insomniac but it really doesn't matter. I take a tape recorder and play tapes in bed, or I put on the wireless. Sometimes I read, but occasionally my eyes hurt....It's frightfully boring not being able to sleep, but it doesn't really hurt one. If I need to, I get up and make cups of tea for myself. I have discovered that I can relax in bed at night, even if I don't sleep very well.

Elaine is now seventy-three. She is not in perfect health — she still has asthma, some bronchitis, and a little rheumatism. She is entitled to a disabled person's sticker for her car.

But mentally and emotionally she has never felt better. She has become good friends with her ex-husband, with whom she often stays. She has many friends. 'I just enjoy life nowadays,' she says.

SEVEN

Stopping Tranquillisers and Sleeping Pills

If you have decided that you may be dependent on your tranquillisers, you will need a plan of action. Getting off these drugs turns out to be surprisingly easy for some lucky women: but for others it is very difficult. A carefully planned series of steps is the best way to come off the pills.

Do not just stop them. Abruptly stopping tranquillisers or sleeping pills can be dangerous. Withdrawals may be unnecessarily severe, or even violent. The correct way to come off the benzodiazepine drugs is to taper them off slowly.

Before starting to do this, you should aim at doing three things.

1. See your doctor and ask his or her help for what you are going to do.

2. Try to get help from a self-help group in your area, or at least have telephone contact with one. There is a list of self-help groups in Appendix 2 of this book.

3. Then *after* you have done this, start reducing the dose — either under the guidance of your doctor, or the self-help group, or following Professor Malcolm Lader's instructions given later in this chapter (page 70 onwards).

Getting your doctor's help

If you have a kindly and up-to-date family doctor, this will not be too difficult. The news that these drugs can be addictive is now beginning to spread, and many general practitioners will at least have *heard* of tranquilliser dependence. The women whose stories appear in this book mostly came off their pills before doctors were even aware of dependence on tranquillisers and sleeping pills.

Some doctors, unfortunately, still cling to the old idea that these pills do not produce drug dependence. In fact, it may well have been your doctor's advice and encouragement that has kept you on the pills all these years. This means you may feel angry; the doctor may well feel uneasy.

Your anger, as well as the doctor's feelings, may make the relationship between you somewhat difficult. At this point, try to keep calm. Remember, your doctor has been misled, often by very persuasive claims, about these drugs. He did not mean to make you drug dependent. He believed that the drugs would do you good. Doctors are human and, like all human beings, can make mistakes in good faith.

If you allow your anger to get the better of you, you will probably make him or her angry too — and you may not get the help you need. So try and be polite, courteous and friendly. Nowadays, most doctors will try to help. But if you have a doctor who cannot admit to a mistake, you may find that he or she is unhelpful.

Tackling your doctor

If you are in doubt about your doctor's attitude, it may help to take along a friend or perhaps your husband or partner for moral support. Write down in advance the reasons why you want to stop the pills, so that if your mind goes blank you can refresh your memory. It may help to take along this book too. The following is a sample dialogue.

You: Hello, doctor. I've come to ask you for some help. You know that I've been taking tranquillisers for the last seven years. Well, I needed them at the beginning, but now I'd like to stop taking them. Can you help me get off them?

Doctor: Why do you want to stop taking them? These pills are very safe drugs, and they seemed to be doing you good.

You: I think I've been taking them too long. They seem to have stopped doing me good. I think they may be harming me. I feel my memory is affected, and I seem to get very vague and depressed. [If you need to, look at the piece of paper where you wrote down the reasons.]

Doctor: You were perfectly happy with them when you first started taking them. I remember you were very anxious and you needed something to help you cope.

You: That's absolutely true, doctor. But I really think I've been on them too long. In fact I am worried that I may be addicted to them.

When you mention addiction to your doctor, you will begin to discover if he or she is up to date or not. If you are lucky, you will find that the doctor is quite receptive to the idea and, if he or she has kept up with medical literature, will then give you instructions on how to taper off the pills.

It is possible, though, that your doctor will be only half informed. In that case, you may get the advice, 'Well, just stop taking the pills'. It cannot be too often stressed — this is *bad* advice. *Do not just stop the pills abruptly.*

You will need to obtain another prescription from your doctor, so that you can taper off the pills slowly. It will probably help if the prescription is for the same strength of drug, but lower milligram tablets. Thus, if you are taking 20 mg a day, ask for 2 mg rather than 5 mg pills.

A third possibility is that at the mention of addiction your doctor will start getting hot under the collar, or even a little cross. You may be told that these are perfectly safe drugs, that you should not question his advice, and that you can take them for years without any worry at all.

Keep calm. Do not argue at this stage. Get a prescription, and leave; you can always try again to get his help. But you now need moral support from elsewhere.

If your doctor is helpful ...
The up-to-date family doctor, on the other hand, nowadays has a planned strategy to help his patients come off their tranquillisers or sleeping pills. Your doctor may give you a sheet of instructions, or he may refer you to a self-help group.

If your doctor gives instructions, it is worth checking that these are really helpful. Tapering off the pills, if you have been on a moderate dose, should take at least a month to six weeks. Occasionally doctors recommend leaving longer intervals between the same-strength pills. This is not the best way. The best way to taper off is to take progressively smaller doses.

If you do have a helpful doctor, this does not mean that

you do not need outside help. Self-help groups offer the kind of warmth and support that no ordinary doctor can. Follow your doctor's medical instructions, but use the group for help and encouragement.

Dealing with an unhelpful doctor
This is a tough one. Some doctors are going to tell you that you must stay on your pills. Are they correct? Are you an individual who will need pills for years?

It is true that some individuals are so crippled with anxiety that being addicted to tranquillisers may be preferable to being without them. At this point it is probably worth your while recalling the original reason for your pills. Was your anxiety extremely severe? Was it severe enough that you had to see a psychiatrist?

If you were so severely anxious that you needed either hospital treatment or a psychiatrist's help, then you may need to be cautious about coming off these pills. The solution is to ask your doctor to refer you back again to the psychiatrist. Discuss the pills with the expert, and make up your mind after hearing what he or she has to say.

Sometimes a doctor will say 'keep taking the pills' without any good reason. The stories of women addicted to tranquillisers show that some doctors are very pill-minded. On the whole, *your* feelings are important in making up your mind about this. It is your body and your mind. If you strongly feel you want to get off the pills, then your opinion is at least as important as the doctor's.

Coming off the pills is basically your decision. No matter how unhelpful your doctor is, you *can* do it. But you are going to need help and advice from elsewhere. Take this help and advice *before* you start reducing the pills.

Self-help groups

Self-help groups give a kind of face-to-face sympathy and encouragement that doctors do not have time to offer. Even the most sympathetic doctor may not understand the difficulties you go through when you come off the pills. But self-help groups will; after all they have done it themselves. There is nothing more encouraging than hearing how somebody else did it. People who have been dependent upon pills understand as nobody else can. They know the dismay, the fear and the despair that you have been feeling when you realized you might be dependent upon the pills. They have struggled with the same feelings.

By now self-help groups are springing up all over the country. Appendix 2 lists the main ones that were operating by the end of 1983. By now there may be new groups in your area. When you get in touch with a group, check that it is made up of people who have been through the same thing, and that some of its members are living a life free from these drugs. Some members of the group will still be coming off the drugs, but if the group is going well there should also be members who can give an example of living without drugs.

Get in touch with a group by phone or letter. Wait to hear from them before you start reducing your drugs. Some groups give instruction sheets on how to proceed. They may even suggest that you go back to your doctor to get his consent before coming off the drugs. The exact procedures within groups vary.

Some women are too shy, too proud, or too 'respectable' to ask for help from these groups. They may be scared off by the words used. They may feel they don't want to be labelled 'an addict' or, if they drink as well as take pills, labelled 'alcoholic'. Yet accepting these labels may be part of getting well. It is only by facing up to drug dependence or addiction, that you can recover from it. Remember that it is an illness, not a vice.

Being courageous enough to ask for help is often the first step to recovery. Without that step, you risk staying ill and becoming worse. If you are to break the vicious circle of drug dependence, you need to start fighting back against the illness. This takes courage. But most women *are* courageous. Your health and happiness matter. Take courage, and start the fight against the pills.

Working out a withdrawal plan

If you are lucky, you will have been given a withdrawal either by your doctor or by your self-help group. Start using it, and try to stick to the instructions.

If you have no withdrawal plan, then you can use one worked out by Professor Malcolm Lader for this book. On the whole, Professor Lader feels that it is best to taper off the drugs fairly fast — in weeks rather than months. 'A longer withdrawal may simply be prolonging the agony,' he says. His withdrawal times is a *minimum*-time plan. Do *not* go any faster.

Tapering off a normal-anxiety dose

If you are taking a dose which is for normal anxiety or insomnia, then take at least a month to taper off. The dose for normal anxiety with diazepam (Valium) is up to 15 mg a day. So if you are taking 15 mg or less a day then follow this plan.

Some of the drugs on the drug chart on page 25 just give the one dose. They do not distinguish between a dose for normal anxiety and one for severe anxiety. If you are taking one of these drugs, then follow the monthly tapering-off schedule if you are on a dose which is less than the maximum.

For instance, instructions for taking the drug clobazam simply suggest a daily total of between 20 to 30 mg. There is no recommended dose for severe anxiety. In this case, follow the monthly tapering-off schedule if you are on up to 20 mg. If you are taking more than this, up to 30 mg, then follow the longer tapering-off schedule, page 71.

To follow the monthly tapering-off schedule, divide the dose by five and reduce by a fifth each week. For instance, if you are taking 15 mg of diazepam (Valium) divide that by five. This means that the first week you take 4 mg three times daily, the second week 3 mg three times daily — and so on.

The easiest way to do this is to ask your doctor for 2 mg instead of 5 mg tablets. The first week you take three doses of two 2 mg tablets. The second week you break one of the tablets in half and take 1½ tablets three times a day. You reduce the dose by half a 2 mg tablet each week, still taking your tablets three times daily as before.

If you cannot get the dose in 2 mg tablets, then you will have to start breaking up the pills. For instance, to get a 4 mg dose of a 5 mg tablet, the easiest way would be first to halve the tablet. Put one half aside, ready to take. Then break the other half into two unequal parts, one larger than the other. The first week take the half, plus the *larger* quarter. The second week take the half, plus the *smaller* quarter.

The exact schedule you follow will partly depend on what kind of tablets you are taking. The principle is to keep the times of the doses as before, but gradually to reduce how much you take. Some people will have to break up their tablets into small crumbs. One way to do this is to use a nailfile to file them down to the right size.

The most difficult pills to manage are the capsules. Ask your doctor if he can prescribe the drug in pill form instead of capsule form. If this is not possible, then you will have to undo the capsule, pour out the powder, divide this up into the right proportions, then put back the amount you need into the capsule and swallow it.

Tapering off a severe-anxiety dose

If you are taking a dose for severe anxiety or severe insomnia, then you need to reduce the dose more slowly over *a minimum of six weeks*.

For instance, if you are taking more than 15 mg of diazepam (Valium), up to 30 mg daily, you need to take six weeks to come off them. A patient on a drug whose instructions do not specify specially high doses (see chart, page 25)) should follow the six-week schedule if taking a relatively high 'normal' dose. For instance, the normal dose for clobazam is between 20 and 30 mg. If you are taking more than 20 mg, it is safest to use the six-week schedule.

This may sound rather complicated. But the principle is simple. The *higher* dose you are on, the *longer* you take to wean yourself off it. If in doubt take the slower rather than the faster method.

The mathematics of reducing a dose are not always easy. Once again, if in doubt go more slowly rather than faster; for example, a woman on a dose of 10 mg of diazepam three times a day might decide to drop her dose by 1½ mg each week.

By getting 2 mg instead of 5 mg tablets, the dose could be reduced in the first week to 8½ mg three times daily, down to 7 mg the following week — and so on over six weeks. To work out the daily reduction over six weeks, divide by seven.

Tapering off a high dose

If you are on a dose which is higher than the doses mentioned on the chart on page 25, then you need medical supervision in reducing the dose. For instance, a woman who is taking a total of more than 30 mg of diazepam (Valium) daily is taking more than the recommended dose.

If your family doctor is unhelpful or not interested in helping you, ask if he or she will refer you to an addiction unit or an alcoholic unit. (Alcoholic units normally treat alcoholics, but usually know about tranquilliser dependence too.)

Sometimes a local self-help group knows of sympathetic doctors. If you are trying to come off a high dose, it may be worth changing doctors to find one who will be helpful. Do this before you start reducing the dose. Occasionally a self-help group can unofficially use their influence to find you a bed in an addiction unit or an alcoholic unit. Accept their help.

Those who can afford to pay for private treatment may be able to come off their drugs in a private clinic. But check around, preferably among ex-patients, to make sure it is a good one. There are some mediocre but extremely expensive clinics in this field.

If you can't get help *come off a high dose extremely slowly.*

Coming off more slowly

Professor Malcolm Lader's suggested schedules for coming off these drugs are based on the assumption that it is best to get the whole thing over quickly, rather than prolonging the agony. However, some self-help groups and some doctors suggest a slower approach.

If you are a person who is happier with long drawnout agony rather than the short, sharp shock effect, then you may choose the slower approach. One suggestion is to reduce the dose every two to four weeks by approximately one-eighth of the previous dose. This may suit individuals who prefer a more cautious approach.

As far as we know, it is almost impossible to avoid withdrawal effects no matter how slowly one withdraws. Some medical experts believe the slower approach is somewhat less painful. Others say that it is just as painful, only the pain goes on that much longer.

Having decided on *your* schedule for reducing the dose, make a chart for yourself, or make the dose reductions in your diary.

Do not delay, unless you have a very good reason indeed. There will never be a perfect moment to start withdrawing. Set the starting date as soon as possible, and then just begin.

Once reducing don't go back

Drug dependence is a cunning kind of illness. When you are coming off the pills, you will probably feel much worse than when you were taking your normal dose. Because you are dependent on these drugs, the body is sending messages that you *need* them. You may also find that your mind invents all kinds of excuses for going back to the old dose.

Do not do this. Once you give in to this kind of thinking, you are plunging back into the vicious circle of drug dependence. All the withdrawal pain you have gone through will be wasted. You may temporarily feel better again, but it will be at the expense of actually being ill again.

If you feel you really cannot continue reducing the dose, *halt at the dose you have reached.* Get more help from your doctor or your self-help group. Tell them how terrible you feel. Stay at the dose until your courage and strength return and you can continue downwards.

Do not go back on to a higher dose. You will simply be throwing away the hard-gained reduction you have already won. Besides, increasing and decreasing the dose like a yo-yo may make you feel worse rather than better.

Will I get withdrawal symptoms?

You may be one of the lucky women who do not get any withdrawal symptoms at all, and stop their pills without any difficulty. Others simply suffer a short rebound effect for a few days, and then have no more trouble.

Exactly what proportion of people have withdrawal symptoms is not known. Estimates vary wildly. One estimate is that one in four people have developed dependence on these drugs after only four months of continuous use. Another study, in which people had taken the drug for an average of three years, suggested that just under half of them would get withdrawal symptoms.

Much will depend on how high a dose you have been taking and for how long. In general, the higher the dose and the longer the time you have taken them the more likely you are to experience withdrawal symptoms. Often, those who start to get withdrawal symptoms if they miss a dose or two, continue with the pills. Thus, long-term users will inevitably contain many people who are dependent.

The timing of any withdrawal symptoms will vary with the different drugs. With shorter-acting pills, the withdrawal symptoms come on fast and abruptly. With the long-acting pills, they may take at least three days to appear. Just occasionally, there is a gap of up to two weeks before there are any symptoms.

What to expect in withdrawal symptoms
The symptoms of withdrawal vary enormously between one individual and another. Very few people indeed will have many of these symptoms. Most people will have *some* of them, if they are experiencing withdrawal symptoms at all. *Nobody will have all of them.*

The following list of mental and phsyical symptoms is compiled both from doctors's studies and from the addicts themselves. Some symptoms are very rare indeed, but it seemed worth listing them so that people who get them are not frightened unnecessarily.

Do remember, that if you are experiencing any of these, they are *a sign that you are getting well*. Feeling ill is, paradoxically, a sign of recovery.

Mental symptoms: Anxiety, panic attacks, agitation, restlessness
General fear: of water, about leaving the house, of crowds
Insomnia, strange dreams

A feeling of unreality, of not being a real person
Depression, lack of confidence, despair, suicidal feelings
Irritability, paranoia, a persecuted feeling, a craving for the
drug or a sudden impulse for it, and 'I don't know what I
want' craving
Tiredness, listlessness, lack of interest in sex

Bodily symptoms: Feeling giddy, or that buildings are going
to fall on you, or that the ground is suddenly sloping
Seasickness, nausea, 'jelly legs', dry vomiting
Frequent visits to the lavatory, incontinence
Pains in the joints, leg pains, shoulder pains, pains in neck
and head
Headaches, feeling ill or 'fluey'
Dry throat, throat muscles seized up, difficulty in
swallowing
Metallic taste in the mouth, strange smells
Ringing in the ears, sensitivity to sounds, hearing sounds
that aren't there; pain as a result of hearing sounds
Sensitivity to light, hallucinations, sore eyes, blurred vision
Losing the sense of touch, numbness, or hypersensitivity
to touch
Breathlessness, dribbling, twitching muscles, shaking
Dry hair, falling hair, broken nails
Skin rashes, vaginal soreness, cracks between the toes,
mouth ulcers, gumboils
Sweating, feeling hot then cold, tingling, and pins and
needles.

How long will these symptoms last?
The time they last varies from one person to another. A
rough guide to how long they *might* last can be worked out
from the number of years you have been on the pills. You
must allow *up to* a month of withdrawal symptoms for
every year you took them. Thus a woman on tranquillisers
for five years may have withdrawal symptoms for five
months.

This is only a rough calculation, as much more research is
still needed. Some self-help groups say that some individuals
may have withdrawal symptoms for up to thirty-five days
for each year of taking pills. These calculations are based on

the worst, not the best, expectations.

Most woman say that the first three months are the worst. After that symptoms are less severe. One slightly confusing fact is that the symptoms are not always continuous. Some women who feel their symptoms are in decline have a sudden relapse into severe withdrawal symptoms again for a few days.

Is there anything I can take to stop the withdrawal symptoms?
This is a tricky question. If you are being withdrawn in a hospital or addiction clinic, then you may be given one of the non-benzodiazepine sedatives or beta-blockers to help you through the first few days of withdrawal. Sometimes doctors prescribe antidepressants for women who are severely depressed on withdrawal.

But most drugs that help withdrawal are also themselves addictive. Just as doctors do not always understand about benzodiazepines being addictive, so they may not fully understand this. A rough rule of thumb is not to take *any* pills unless you are being treated by a doctor who fully understands about drug dependence.

Therefore, if you are being treated by a family doctor who is not up to date, you may be offered yet another benzodiazepine drug. Before taking any drugs, it is therefore as well to doublecheck them against the list of benzodiazepines in Chapter 1, pages 9–10.

All the benzodiazepine drugs are interchanageable as far as dependence is concerned. There is really no point in changing from a dependence on say, diazepam, to a dependence on clobazam.

Unfortunately there is no pill or medicine that will help you to come off your tranquillisers without also being potentially addictive. But the good news is that you will only have to go through withdrawal symptoms once. When they are over, you can put all the pain and trouble behind you.

Can I not take the occasional pill?
No, don't. If you are going through withdrawal symptoms there is a great temptation to take just one pill. If you do, you will simply be hooked again.

Tell yourself there is no situation that a pill will make better. You might feel temporarily better with a pill, but you will actually be worse.

Think of all the good things you have to look forward to — a life free from pills, a better memory, a clearer brain, the chance to feel love and happiness of a kind that the pills have taken away from you.

If you take a pill, you are throwing away all that, and going back into the world of deadened feelings. Recall the times that you were forgetful, weepy, or just plain drugged because of the pills. Do you want all that misery back? Because that is what you will get, if you take just one pill.

Coming off pills is not easy. It is a fight against an insidious and painful disease, drug dependence. But women in their hundreds are beginning this fight and if they can succeed, you can do it too.

A special note for women who feel they cannot go through with it — don't give up. Perhaps at the moment you do not feel strong enough to start dealing with your drug dependence. But what you cannot do today, you may find the strength and courage to do tomorrow.

EIGHT

Living without Pills

Now that you have stopped, or are reducing your pills, you will need all the help you can get in the first few weeks. Recovering from drug dependence is not easy. Not only do you have to stop taking pills; you have to stay off them. It means learning to live without the pills as a chemical crutch.

Some outsiders never really understand what drug dependence means. They think it is just a question of throwing away the pill bottle. Getting rid of the pills is a vital part of recovery — but it is not the whole story. It is only the first part.

Anybody who has taking mood-altering pills for a number of years has become used to living with their help. As we have seen, tranquillisers seem to stop helping anxiety after a few months; but they continue to blot out the sharp edges of life. Even nightly sleeping pills can persist in the body throughout the day, making life slightly blurred at the edges. Women who have been taking these drugs in high doses have been living for months or years in what is almost a permanent fog.

The pills seem to soften the impact of the outside world. They also seem to suppress inner emotions and diminish feelings in general. People on pills may have been living a life where no emotions are really *felt* in a natural way.

The first few weeks of living without pills sometimes takes people by surprise. Not only are there withdrawal symptoms, but there is also the unusual feeling of living life in the raw. It is as if a protective skin has been peeled away leaving the self unusually vulnerable. Even women who have no withdrawal trouble at all may experience this.

As the natural feelings of anger, fear, excitement or even joy occur, there is now no pill to blot them out or to soften their impact. When life does not go smoothly, there is no pill to turn to, to blot out the trouble. These are the danger moments, when a desire to go back on the pills can hit you hard.

A day at a time

The day-at-a-time plan is practised by members of Narcotics Anonymous (and also by Alcoholics Anonymous). It involves trying to live just one day at a time, letting both the past and the future take care of themselves. Living in a watertight compartment of just one day can be a help in getting through the first difficult days of being without pills.

If somebody asked you 'Can you manage just one single day, today, without a tranquilliser?', you would probably agree that you could. It is quite easy to do something for a day. Even very difficult or distressing ordeals are possible just for a single day.

Quite often it is the thought of more than a day which is so worrying. If you knew that your withdrawal symptoms were only going to last for one day, they would not seem nearly so bad. It is the thought of the way they may go on for weeks which is so distressing.

Members of Narcotics Anonymous use the day-at-a-time philosophy as a kind of mental trick. They concentrate all their efforts on not taking a drug just for the twenty-four hours in which they are living. They give up drugs 'just for one day', rather than swearing off for a lifetime. But as each new day dawns, they commit themselves again to the present twenty-four hours. In this way the single days add up into weeks, months and years.

Many women who are dependent upon their pills are frightened to stop taking them, because they are looking forward to a horrifying picture of life without pills. How shall I manage the weeks of sleeplessness? What will I do at my daughter's wedding next month? How shall I manage the bad days at the office? How can I get through those days when my husband's in a temper, my teenage son is grumpy and the cat's sick?

If you look again at these worries, you will see that they all have one thing in common — they are all worries about the future. But if you are thinking only of what the day itself brings, these worries do not apply. You can save your energy and strength to deal with what is happening today, now — not what will happen in the future.

The other thought that plagues women who are giving up their drugs is the past. Why should I be the one to get addicted? Is it my fault that I asked for tranquillisers in the first place? Does this mean I am psychologically weak? Why don't I have the strength of mind to stop easily? Some women may be tormented by the thoughts of how vague and odd they were when under the influence of the drugs.

Thoughts about the past like these have no place in the day-at-a-time plan. Guilt about what you did, anger about the doctor, or feelings of self-pity about how unfair it is — these are all feelings about the past. In the day-at-a time plan they are simply passed through and out of the mind. What matters is *now*.

Practising this way of living for the day is not easy. So often the worries about the future or the fears about the past come into you mind without your noticing. That is why self-help groups can be so useful. People can remind you that you are letting future worries or past guilts torment you unnecessarily.

Bad moments — the minutes-at-a-time emergency plan

In the first few weeks of stopping or reducing the pills, you may have moments when you feel you just cannot stand any more of it. There will be surges of bad feelings — despair, panic, fear or even wild anger.

At these moments you may also have cravings for the drug. There may be an intense feeling of *needing* it, a deceptively idle desire just to take one, or a sudden impulse for one. Sometimes the craving is not so much *for* the drug, as for an end to the unpleasant withdrawal feelings. There may even be what one ex-addict describes as 'I-don't-know-what-I-want feeling but I want *something*'.

Just because you feel this way does not mean that you *have* to take the pill. The most overwhelming feelings can be lived through. Let them pour through your mind but do not act on them.

At moments like this asking yourself if you can live through just one day without the drug may well get the answer 'No'. So reduce the day-at-a-time plan to a minutes-at-a-time plan.

Tell yourself that you will live through the next ten minutes without the drug. Postpone taking the pill for that ten minutes. When the ten minutes is up, start getting through the next ten minutes without the drug. 'Just for ten minutes I will hold out without it' is what you tell yourself.

This mental trick usually sees people through the worst moments safely. After a couple of hours, their hope and strength return so that they can go back on the day-at-a-time plan. It *does* work. With the help of this mental trick from Narcotics Anonymous thousands of addicts have given up their drugs and stayed off them.

Putting your drug problem first

Every woman in the world has anxieties and responsibilities. She may have a demanding job outside the home, a family to organize. There are probably job or money worries, difficulties with children, disagreements with a partner, elderly relatives to care for, and many other responsibilities.

The trick in recovering from dependence on tranquillisers is to put this particular problem first. Imagine a list of your problems. Your tranquilliser difficulty might well come third or fourth on the list. Put it at the top, even if it doesn't *seem* the most important, and tackle it *first*.

If you can get off tranquillisers, you will be better placed to cope with the other problems, for although taking the pills makes people apparently feel better, it has been proved that actually the pills make them less able to cope. If you are free from pills and clear-headed all the other problems on your list will be easier to deal with.

Let us take an example. Suppose that your most important worry is money. You are overdrawn at the bank. You do not know how to get extra money. You feel this is the worst of your problems — much worse than the fact that you are also dependent on tranquillisers.

Stop for a moment and think it out. Perhaps the money difficulties *are* worse. But if you give priority to your tranquilliser problem, dealing with that *first*, you will be in a better position to deal with the money troubles. Being clear-headed, you will be able to think of ways to raise money, to talk to the bank manager clearly, perhaps to get yourself together enough to find a better job.

If you don't put your tranquilliser problem first, postpone getting off them until the money difficulties are sorted out, what will happen? This will mean months longer on the pills and worse withdrawal symptoms when eventually you *do* come off them. And perhaps you will even allow your money worries to put you back on the pills. How will that help you? It won't. All that it will do is to make you forgetful and drugged at a time when you need all your brain power and energies to solve your money difficulties.

So putting your tranquilliser problem first, and dealing with it, really does make good sense.

Women sometimes find this particularly difficult to do. Society encourages them to live for and through others, putting their own needs second. If you have spent the past five or more years blunting your own feelings with pills, you may be in the habit of thinking that other people's needs are more important than your own.

This is false kindness. You *must* give your time and your energy to your own problem, tranquilliser dependence. In the long run nobody is going to thank you if you stay ill under the false idea that you must now inconvenience others. Your first duty is to look after your own health and sanity; it is only when we are well and happy that we can truly help others.

Talk to yourself

It may seem odd to recommend talking to yourself as an aid to recovery. People make jokes about this habit, even saying that talking to oneself is the first sign of madness.

However, if you are coming off tranquillisers, talking to yourself may be one of the first signs of recovery. Give yourself the encouragement and help you need — either out loud or at least inside your head. Psychologists recommend this as a valuable therapeutic technique.

Talking to yourself also helps you think right. Tranquilliser dependence has a psychological side to it. Your mind, as well as your body, has been accustomed to these drugs.

As part of coming off the drugs, the mind may start inventing excuses why you should go back on them.

You can counterattack with thoughts of your own. Think of all the bad things about your tranquilliser dependence. Recall the deadened feelings you had. Try to recollect the times when the pills stopped your functioning. Paint a picture in your mind of all the misery and pain these drugs have caused you. Use this picture for the moments when you have a craving to take a pill.

Another psychological ploy to help is thinking about life without drugs. Tell yourself about all the good things you have to look forward to, once the withdrawal symptoms are over. You will have a better memory, a clearer brain, a chance to feel love and happiness of a kind that the pills seemed to damp down. Promise yourself a bright future.

Talking yourself through bad moments

Many people suffer panic attacks when they first come off pills. Or they have moments of unreasonable fear, self-consciousness, or embarrassment. Talking to yourself, either aloud or silently, can help you live through these moments.

Some people find that repeating a phrase over and over again is helpful. Narcotics Anonymous use their adopted prayer: 'God give me the serenity to accept the things I cannot change, courage to change the things I can, and wisdom to know the difference'.

Non-believers may find this idea rather offputting. But it is well worth trying all the same — using perhaps a quotation or even just a phrase that means something to you. The point is that the repetition of a few words seems to calm the mind, and helps it move out of its emotional turmoil. It changes the focus away from the fear to the words themselves.

Those who enjoy poetry may find a verse that will help them. Some people repeat whole poems to themselves, not because of what the poems *say*, but because the effort of remembering the words deflects the mind. Christians may find repeating the 23rd psalm helpful.

Do it gently

Be kind to yourself. Coming off pills is not easy. For the first few weeks at least you are not going to be at your best. Do not expect too much of yourself. Treat yourself gently. Give yourself the tender loving care that you would give others if they were ill.

The first few weeks and months without pills need careful treatment by yourself. This is not a time to pick up extra burdens, just the reverse. Do not undertake any major projects in the first six months to a year of coming off pills. Postpone any new responsibilities for that time, if possible.

Postpone major decisions too, if you can. When you come off pills your mind and body are likely to be in some turmoil. This is not the time to make major changes to your life — taking a new job, leaving your husband, getting married, starting a new baby. There will be time for these later, when you have recovered from the withdrawal symptoms.

Do not be afraid to let things slide if necessary. Ask yourself 'Is it that important?' Usually it isn't. For a few weeks the family can put up with a bit of mess and untidiness. The odd take away meal won't hurt them. Take time off work, if you need it.

Drug dependence is an illness, and in recovering you need the same care that recovering from any illness requires. You need to nurse yourself along a bit.

Take your time in everything you do, even little household chores. Accept help from other people — if they don't offer, ask for it.

Keep busy

Although you need to take things slowly, don't just stop all activity. Just sitting doing nothing and brooding about your symptoms will only make you feel much worse. You need something to do to keep yourself occupied.

This is the time for light and easy tasks — cleaning your shoes, light housework, making a simple cake slowly with pleasure, hoovering, taking the dog for a walk, doing some light gardening.

Do not throw yourself into heavy physical work when you come off the pills. Tranquillisers are muscle relaxants, and sometimes the muscles seize up when the pills are withdrawn. Heavy digging in the garden or heavy work of any kind can lead to muscle spasm and pain.

If you go out to work, these first few weeks are time for doing routine tasks, rather than new projects. Coast along a bit till you begin to feel better. One woman coming off tranquillisers used to lock her office door, and lie down flat on the floor for ten minutes to relax. There is always the ladies' lavatory to retreat to, if you have a bad attack of panic.

Self-help groups

The first few weeks of coming off pills are much easier if you have people to talk to. This is where self-help groups are so vital. The other women and men in them know what you are going through; they have been through the same things themselves.

Groups often offer the kind of 24-hour support that even a truly caring doctor cannot. Often members swap phone numbers so that they can ring each other at dark moments. Pick up the phone and talk to somebody instead of letting the fear and misery pile up. Do this whenever you need to.

It is best to try and meet other sufferers face to face. Most self-help groups offer this kind of contact. But if there is no group near you, you can at least telephone one for help and advice. When you feel emotionally strong enough, and over the worst of the withdrawal symptoms, you could try starting your own group in your area.

Sometimes family and friends are not as helpful as they might be. Some husbands are impatient, even unkind, to their wives about their tranquilliser problem; children may lack understanding. They may be unwilling to listen to you, or even uncaring about your difficulties.

Do not let anybody else's behaviour alter your determination to give up pills. After all, you are doing this for your *own* sake. If you let somebody else's reactions push you back on the pills, who will suffer? Only you.

Even if your family does try to be helpful you may find that they cannot fully understand what you are going through. That is why most people need help from fellow sufferers. After the first few weeks you may find that even normally loving family members get a bit bored with constant talk about tranquillisers. Yet talking out the problem may be something you badly need.

Many women have feelings and thoughts that need bringing into the open. They may want to rethink much of their life, and the way it has been going, in the light of their drug dependence. A self-help group normally provides conditions in which you can do that.

Should I tell outsiders?

This is an individual decision. There are two extremes. Some women are so afraid of being labelled an addict, that they dare not tell anyone — and consequently cut themselves off from the love and help they need. Others are just the reverse. They buttonhole almost anybody and want to tell them about it. They may start a little crusade to stop anybody they know taking these pills! This can produce ill-feeling among even close friends.

It is probably best to aim at the middle course. Tell those whom you love — family and friends. They will probably show their love by help and encouragement.

Occasionally you may get a shock. A friend you thought might sympathize may turn a cold shoulder. Perhaps she is dependent on pills herself and finds it uncomfortable to hear how you have given them up. Perhaps she was just a fair-weather friend. Just drop the subject with her (or drop *her*).

Many women wonder if they should tell people at work. It has to be a personal decision — but, *if in doubt, don't*. While you are going through withdrawal, you will find it difficult to exercise good judgement, and may make the wrong decision. The best way is to be cautious.

Unfortunately our society does not understand about drug dependence — least of all dependence on tranquillisers. If you tell the authorities at work, you may find it is put down as a black mark against your future prospects. *You* know that coming off the drug will make you a better worker and a more valuable employee. They may simply think of you as 'that woman on pills'.

Of course, *friends* at work are something different. It will help if there is a close friend somewhere in the office or the works in whom you can confide.

Get help from other sources

If you are offered help from anywhere else, grab it with both hands. Your doctor may refer you elsewhere — to a social worker, a counsellor or a psychologist. Accept gratefully.

Sometimes there are other sources of help — community associations, church groups, or women's groups. If you have a religion, use its resources; you may find a minister or vicar is a help, and you will be helping him look out for others with the same trouble. Feminists will often find love and support from their local women's groups.

The other source of love and affection in many women's lives is a pet. If you own a dog or a cat, these companionable animals will comfort you through difficult times. Giving the dog a good cuddle, or spending time stroking the cat may help you during panic attacks. We live in a world which often sneers at the love and affection that animals give us. Yet this affection is a healing thing. Research has proved how valuable the love of animals is for human beings. You need not be ashamed of it.

Dependence upon drugs is sometimes described as 'a disease of isolation'. Drugs cut us off from human feelings and real relationships. Anything that gives us love and affection and enables us to feel these again will help the healing process.

Look after yourself

It is no good pretending that there is any magic to blot out the pain of the first few weeks without drugs. There is not. However, sensible care for yourself will help you cope.

Eat properly at regular mealtimes, and have at least three good meals a day. Some self-help groups feel that five small meals a day are better. Take plenty of fresh fruit, wholemeal bread, and vegetables. If you find it difficult to prepare proper meals for yourself, see if you can persuade a family member to take over some of the cooking.

You may find that when you stop taking pills, you have a craving for chocolate. Why not? Of course, too much chocolate is not very good for you, but if it helps for the first few weeks, then eat it. Put a bar of chocolate in your handbag for difficult moments. For those who find chocolate only makes them sick an apple in the handbag might help.

Take a multivitamin preparation daily if you want to, but don't go over the top with vitamins. It is possible to overdose dangerously with some vitamins, so read the instructions and stick to them. Health store vitamins are no better than vitamins from the chemist, and are usually more expensive.

Tea and coffee are stimulants and sometimes make people feel even more agitated. Some soft drinks, especially cola drinks, have caffeine in them. Give up these drinks if you feel agitated and restless, and take fruit juices, decaffeinated coffee, lemon and honey instead. Malted milky drinks are comforting last thing at night.

Take gentle exercise. If you are suffering from agoraphobia, get a friend or family member to help you go out for short walks. Get help with shopping trips too — start by short journeys to the local shops, then work up to the local supermarket.

While you are suffering withdrawal symptoms, don't drive or operate heavy machinery as your coordination and concentration may be affected. Wait until you feel better before you start using the car.

Keep a diary

Sometimes this helps people get through the blackest moment. If you are keeping a diary of your symptoms and feelings, remember to put down any day — or any hour — in which you felt joyful, happy or peaceful. Then in the black moments of despair, you can remember that you *have* had moments of relief. It may also be encouraging to see how you are progressing.

Night-time and insomnia

Insomnia is one of the most common withdrawal symptoms in people coming off tranquillisers or sleeping pills. There is rebound insomnia when you stop taking sleeping pills, even if you have only been on them a few days. If you are having proper withdrawal symptoms, this insomnia may continue for some time.

Accept it. Live through it. These sleepless nights are part of your recovery. They may be hell to live through, but it helps if you think of them as a sign of recovery. Insomnia, even complete nights without any sleep at all, has never killed anybody.

If you are married, it will be a good idea temporarily to move out of the double bed into the spare room. Take with you plenty of non-stimulating books — harmless romances rather than exciting thrillers. Read them through the night, if necessary.

Make sure you keep warm. A hot water bottle, bedsocks, a bed jacket, and an electric blanket are all helpful. Some people find heated electric pads better than hot water bottles. If you are finding the long hours dreary, get up and make yourself a little snack or a milky drink.

The trick in dealing with this withdrawal insomnia is simply to live through it. Worrying about it will make you feel worse. Sleepless nights do least harm when the person tries to relax during the long hours of not sleeping.

Be careful about other drugs

During withdrawal, be extra careful about taking any kind of drug, even harmless ones sold over the counter. There is a slight risk, but a risk nonetheless, that you may be tempted into becoming dependent on something else. Occasionally people stopping drugs turn to other pills or to alcohol for relief from the withdrawal symptoms, and thereby risk developing a new dependence.

As the last chapter made clear, be careful that a well-meaning but out-of-date doctor does not offer you tranquillisers or sleeping pills again. If you take any of these pills you are simply risking dependence all over again, and you might have to go through withdrawal twice.

The benzodiazepine drugs are also sometimes given to people as muscle relaxants for back pain. They are given in injections before dental treatment, and before hospital operations. Ask a doctor or dentist what they are giving you.

Many doctors of course, are irritated by patients who do this. But it is *your* life and health at risk, and you are fully entitled to ask them. It is better to have five minutes rudeness from a doctor, than risk dependence and withdrawal all over again. Also, though he or she may not like the idea, you will be educating your doctor.

Some doctors, well-meaning medical men and women who do not specialize in addiction, have the idea that after a certain period off the drug it is safe for people to take the pills again. Normally, the only safe rule for anybody who became dependent on a drug, is *never* to take that drug again. *Just one pill* carries the risk of drug dependence again, with all the attendant problems of withdrawal. If you have been lucky enough to escape the lion's den, you don't go back inside to retrieve your hat.

NINE

Learning to Live with Anxiety

Anxiety has a natural part in most people's lives. To feel anxious is appropriate to some occasions; it is also very common sometimes to feel more anxiety than is necessary. Any normal person will feel anxious about an approaching dentist's appointment, a job interview, an examination or a hospital operation. A person who felt no anxiety about these would be extraordinary indeed.

But many women suffer *more* anxiety than they need — especially if they have been used to living on tranquillisers. At first they experience the pangs of either rebound or withdrawal anxiety, then even after withdrawal they probably feel unaccustomed feelings of worry. After all, for months and years they have used pills to damp down feelings. Now, without the pills, these emotions may feel raw and unexpectedly strong.

Nobody should aim at a life without anxiety. That would be unnatural and inhuman. We should aim at living *with* anxiety, but living in such a way that the feelings of worry, though they are there, are not strong enough to interfere with ordinary life.

People vary in their anxiety levels. Some individuals are naturally happy-go-lucky, and do not even fret about grave problems. Others seem natural worriers. Even when their life is going quite smoothly, they will find something to worry about.

However, even natural worriers can take steps to deal with their anxious feelings; they don't just suffer. They can at least aim at diminishing the strength of anxiety, and try to lead a happy life despite the feelings.

Do alternative methods actually work?

Some alternative methods of reducing anxiety have been tested and found to work; others have not been tested at all.

But even the methods that have been tested do not provide the instant relief of anxiety which a pill gives.

Pills work very well indeed — at the beginning. If you take a tranquilliser, you will feel your anxiety beginning to diminish. If you take a sleeping pill, you will soon fall into a drugged slumber. But after several weeks, the effects of the pills being to wear off. Some people need higher doses, and this increases the risk of drug dependence.

Alternative methods of coping with anxiety have just the opposite effect. At the beginning they do not work very well. But as the weeks pass, they begin to work better. For instance, the first time you attend a relaxation class you may not feel much better at all. But as you continue attending classes and practising relaxation techniques, their effect becomes stronger. And, unlike pills, there is no risk of drug dependence.

Relaxing — body and mind

Relaxation is a two-fold affair. 'Anxiety involves several response systems. There's the physical side, the way the body behaves, and there's the mental side, the way the mind behaves,' says psychologist Joe Ruzek of Drinkwatchers, who is also an adviser to the self-help group Tranx.

> Some people have bodily symptoms of anxiety without knowing it; others feel anxious but do not show it in their bodies. You really need to tackle anxiety on several fronts....You can learn physical methods of relaxation and, if you practise them, they in turn may affect the mind. Then you can tackle the mental side of anxiety with techniques which in turn will affect the body.

Relaxing the body
Most of the physical relaxation techniques are more easily practised in groups than alone. You can buy relaxation tapes, and books giving relaxation exercises (see Appendix 2, page 118), but these are easier to persist with if you have fellow relaxers.

Deep breathing is one of the relaxation techniques taught at the Tranquilliser Withdrawal Support Group in Newcastle in Northumberland. Some women feel breathless when they first stop taking the pills, so deep breathing is particularly useful for the first few weeks of withdrawal. It is also a good technique for handling stressful moments.

When people are upset, angry, frightened or anxious they often unconsciously start to breathe quickly, a shallow kind of breathing rather like panting. This involves the upper part of the lungs. In deep breathing you breathe from the lower part of the lungs with the stomach moving rather than the upper chest.

The usefulness of deep breathing is that it can be practised almost anywhere. Are you tense and upset in the office? Two or three moments of deep breathing can help relax you. Probably nobody will even notice you while you do it.

The best way to start is to practise deep breathing for five to ten minutes daily, to get into the rhythm of doing it. Lie on the floor, putting one hand on your chest and one on your stomach. Breathe out. Then take a long breath in. If you are deep breathing, your hand over your tummy will rise before the hand on your chest. If your chest is rising first, then your breathing is shallow. Practise until your tummy is rising before your chest, and rising proportionately higher than your chest.

Other more complicated relaxation techniques are probably best practised in a class. Local adult education centres often offer relaxation classes. Yoga classes also offer techniques which aid relaxation. For those who can afford higher fees, the Alexander Technique, usually taught in one-to-one sessions, may be helpful.

Whichever types of physical relaxation exercise you pursue, remember that the benefits will not be immediately apparent. You must persist for several weeks, until you are practising the technique easily and skilfully. Then you may find that physical relaxation starts helping you towards not just a relaxed body but a quieter mind.

Exercise — a way to relax

Physical exercise is not usually thought of as relaxing. But it is. There is nothing better for insomnia than the natural tiredness brought on by physical exertion. Exercise aids the mind too. It is extraordinarily difficult to keep worrying about something, if you are trying to play a good game of tennis or a round of golf. Exercise occupies the mind just enough to give it a rest from anxiety.

It is important to choose some kind of exercise that you enjoy. Doggedly pursuing some kind of game which you do not like will simply be counterproductive. If you have given up your pills, this is a good time to take up a new sport — jogging, golf, tennis, swimming, aerobic dancing or horse riding.

Nowadays most sports have as many older members as younger ones. Pensioners can be found doing dancing classes, learning how to swim and even taking part in jogging marathons. If you are not the traditionally sporting type, then consider the less obvious exercise of walking, bird-watching, or perhaps gardening. Getting a dog may help the elderly to take at least two short walks a day.

But do not start exercising abruptly. Women who have been on tranquillisers report that they sometimes suffer muscular spasm or even back trouble if they do too much too soon. It is, anyway, a good general rule for any exercise to take it easily in the beginning. Work up slowly towards strenuous exercises. If you are elderly or in poor health, check with your doctor first.

Joe Ruzek says:

> One of the benefits of exercise is that you feel good, and your self-esteem goes up....It may also help those who suffer from heart palpitations and overbreathing during anxiety. After exercise, your heart pounds and you take heavy breaths quite naturally. By experiencing this, people will realize that these symptoms are not always bad.

Meditation for physical relaxation

Meditation as a relaxation technique has been shown to work. A British doctor treated patients with high blood pressure by persuading them to carry out twenty minutes of meditation and relaxation twice a day. Compared with patients who were not doing this, their blood pressure droped quite markedly.

Meditation is another technique which is more easily learned in groups. Some people just worry all the more, if they sit down and try to meditate 'cold'. The best-known way to learn meditation is by learning from various oriental groups teaching Transcendental or Siddha yoga meditation.

The principles of meditation is usually to have some kind of mental device — a mantra, a single word, or a visual picture. The mind is concentrated upon this in such a way as to blot out distracting or worrying thoughts. When this is done, the body also relaxes.

If you are uncomfortable with oriental religions, then you may find that your own Christian church has a meditation organization somewhere. If you wish to meditate in the company of others, then Quaker meetings are largely devoted to silent prayer. Quakers welcome everybody, including non-Christians and even atheists to their meetings. It might be worth trying one of these.

Relaxing the mind

It would be wrong to suggest that anxiety can be easily managed merely by a series of physical exercises and mental tricks. These do help, but are probably least effective for people in whom an anxious response is deeply ingrained. Some women have learned anxiety as a way of responding to life. Changing that response is going to be difficult.

One suggestion is that you should try to find out what triggers off your anxiety. This involves keeping a monthly diary in which you record every occasion on which you felt anxious or tense. Was it before social occasions like parties or coffee mornings? Was it in the office? Was it when you had to talk to your husband about bills?

The kind of detail you need to note is not just *when* you feel anxious, but also how. What does your mind *say* to you when you feel worried? For instance, if you feel anxious before a social occasion, you may be saying to yourself 'I am afraid I shall make a fool of myself with these people....I am not really an interesting person so nobody will want to talk to me...now that I am in my forties nobody will like me because I am no longer young'.

Writing down this kind of detail is not easy. It takes time and considerable thought. You may even feel a bit of a fool as you fill out whole exercise books on the subject.

Nevertheless, it is well worth doing. When you have

finished your whole month's diary, put it aside for at least a week and do not look at it. Then, when you have a spare hour or so, reread it. Underline the significant moments when you notice anxiety repeating itself. Have a careful look at what your mind seems to be saying on these anxious occasions.

If you can find some pattern of events and thoughts in the diary, you are well on the way to dealing with the problem. What occasions make you anxious? What sort of worrying thoughts go through your head?

Training yourself to cope

Suppose you have found, from your diary, that it is social occasions you find so worrying. What is more, you have noticed that your thoughts seem to be along the lines of feeling unlovable, uninteresting or boring. Your mind is telling you that you are not going to enjoy such occasions, and that you *do not deserve to.*

At this point, you need to start planning a series of lessons for yourself. You are going to train yourself on social occasions, so that after some practice you can manage them without undue anxiety.

Do not start with large occasions. Start by accepting the least important social occasion you can think of. For instance, invite just one friend to coffee. Then begin practising on larger occasions. Go to a coffee morning, or a party. Treat each occasion not as a treat, but as a *practice event*. The aim is not to be the most swinging woman at the party — it is simply to be there and to try out various techniques.

Re-programme your thoughts about such occasions. Instead of telling yourself how worrying it will be if you do something wrong, tell yourself how it doesn't matter if you fall over in the middle of the room. Tell yourself how very interesting you are going to find the *others*. Tell yourself how they are really just like you. Tell yourself, above all, that you were invited because they *want you to be there*. You are a wanted guest.

As each occasion is going to be a kind of practice run, try to plan some of it in advance. Put on your best and brightest makeup, and your prettiest clothes. Smile at people. Work out one or two remarks to say. Practise these in front of the mirror. Remember, you are interested in *people*. *Pretend* to be interested. Sometimes a pretence, if practised hard, can become a reality.

This sort of self-training can be applied to almost anything. Firstly identify the problem. Then set up a gradual schedule of practice events — starting with the easiest and slowly working up to the most difficult. Treat each event merely as a practice occasion, but plan it all out beforehand.

Problem-solving

Some people have a particular reason to be anxious. They have real problems in their life — financial difficulties, health difficulties, relationship difficulties.

Psychologists like Joe Ruzek recommend trying a problem-solving technique for this. First, write down what really is the problem. Then write down twenty ways of dealing with it, even ways that seem rather silly. Make this a kind of brainstorming session.

For instance, if you have a bank overdraft, write down twenty ways of doing something about it — for example, getting a part-time job for extra money, seeing the bank manager, borrowing money from relatives, taking a second mortgage.

Add other ideas, even high-flown ones like winning the pools or finding buried treasure. The point about these silly ideas is to get your brain working freely on the problem. Let it look into *every* possibility, so that it may find answers it has ignored up till now.

When you have listed all the solutions you can think of, look through them all. Pick out the best one and do it. If this fails, then try a second solution.

Altering attitudes

We cannot choose the circumstances in which we live. We cannot guard our lives against accidents, misfortunes, or even tragedies. If the country's economy goes downhill and we are sacked, we cannot singlehandedly do anything about it. If a relation dies in a road accident, we are powerless to stop it happening. Life is full of incidents and accidents which are set into motion despite our wishes.

But we are free to choose our *response* to such accidents. We cannot choose the hand of cards life deals out to us, but we can decide how to play them. We have the power to change our attitudes. We can choose to be happy and grateful for the good things in our lives, or we can choose to be miserable and full of self-pity about the bad things.

Unfortunately many women, and many men too, have developed attitudes of mind which do not make them happy. These attitudes are often ingrained ways of looking at things, or responding to events, which may not even be obvious to the person who has them. Yet they are there.

Take, for instance, the perfectionist. A perfectionist attitude is one that requires too much not only of others, but also of oneself. The perfectionist wants everything to be just so all the time. Naturally she is often disappointed.

The perfectionist expects a lot of herself. Perhaps she is the perfect housewife who works night and day to keep her house absolutely spotless. She expects a lot of others too. She is always nagging the family about being neat — or she cleans up after them, a martyr all the way. She complains about slaving away in the house and the thoughtlessness of others.

The problem is not her housework or her family. The problem is her own perfectionist expectations. One way of making her life happier would be to drop this particular attitude, expect less from herself and others, and be content with a slightly messy house. If she can do this, she will be more content.

Other attitudes which hurt people are self-pity, anger, fear, self-obsession, pride and its companion insecurity, and trying to control others. These attitudes actually hurt the person who holds them. It is impossible to be angry and happy at the same time. It is impossible to be both full of self-pity and happy.

Changing attitudes is not at all easy, Many people refuse even to try. They say they are angry perhaps, because other people treat them badly — thus justifying their own attitudes. They cannot see that they are hurting themselves. But changing attitudes is possible. For those who have the courage and persistence to try, it can be very rewarding.

Worrying for others

One particular attitude which is common among women is anxiety on behalf of others. It is not the same as having sympathy and compassion for others. Worrying for others goes further.

The worrier often takes over other people's burdens. Suppose a relation tells her of some unhappiness, the worrier does not just listen and sympathize. She take over the unhappiness and carries it around as if it was her own. She will probably fuss round for several days, anxiously asking if things have got better, making all kinds of suggestions, even telling the person how unhappy it has made *her* feel.

Often people stop telling her their troubles. Most of us know men and women who dare not tell their wives or mothers or sisters if something goes wrong. They dread the fuss that will be made — or they dread the way their womenfolk will start worrying about it. 'I didn't tell you,' they explain later, 'because I knew it would worry you.'

In fact, these worriers are not much use to their friends and family because of their habit of unnecessarily picking up other people's burdens. Sometimes the worrier prides herself on her sympathy. But other people see her sympathetic worrying more as a trouble than a help.

This kind of worry has been described as 'an exaggerated sense of responsibility'. And these worriers are not extra-kind sensitive people but, oddly enough, rather egotistical.

Changing a habit of worrying for others will help diminish some of the anxiety in life. Learn to develop the art of letting go of a problem. If a person confides her unhappiness to you, be kind to her, listen, and then forget about it.

Sometimes it helps to ask yourself: 'Can I *do* anything about this?' For instance, if an elderly relative is in hospital for a serious operation, write her a note or visit her. But do not lie awake all night worrying about it. You have done what you can; the rest is in other people's hands.

Accept that there are things in life you cannot change; they must just be accepted. Fighting about them, worrying about them or wasting time brooding on them simply wastes energy.

Enrich your life

Stopping tranquillisers is for many people something of an ordeal. But it can also be the start of something good in life. Use this difficult moment to make a new start. Renew your life and enrich it.

Some people find that when they stop their pills, they have unfinished business from the past. Anita Gordon, who runs Tranx Release in Northampton, was one of these. She had been given tranquillisers to help her through a divorce, and then gone on taking them for years.

When she stopped taking her pills, she had been happily remarried for nearly fourteen years. Yet thoughts of her first marriage and her divorce seemed to come surging back. 'I didn't know what had happened,' she says, 'Then when I told my husband, he said "Let's talk about it."'

Other women have had similar experiences. Women who were given tranquillisers to help them over the death of a baby find they have to go through a period of mourning for the child when they come off the pills. Widows may find they need to mourn their lost husbands — maybe years later. The unfinished business from the past has to be worked through.

Sometimes the unfinished business is a truly difficult situation. Pills may have helped you put up with a job you do not enjoy, live with a person who you do not love. Without the pills, you may have to reconsider these choices. Sometimes it will mean taking the plunge and changing the job or even leaving an unhappy marriage.

This is the moment to reassess your life, once you have got through the withdrawals and are feeling well again. Where do you want to go in life? Which parts of your life need improvements? Are there changes you need to make? Do you want to change direction?

Use the new life to make these changes. Take up the hobbies you dropped while you were under the influence of tranquillisers. Break the unhappy marriage that dragged on because you were too ill to change it — or begin to work on improving that marriage so it becomes the sort of relationship you want. Start training for a job you always wanted. Go back to evening classes. Learn something new. Make something beautiful.

More about sleep

After the insomnia of the withdrawal period, some people find that their sleeping pattern becomes quite normal. Others remain insomniacs to a lesser or greater degree. Once the withdrawal period is over, you can begin to try and do something about your insomnia.

The relaxation techniques learned in class can often be practised while lying in bed at night, as can meditation. There are also a number of very good books about sleep which are worth consulting (see Appendix 2, page 118)

One way to aid sleep is to give up all coffee, tea and soft drinks which contain caffeine. Give up smoking too. These are all stimulants which might be contributing to your insomnia.

Regularize your life. A thoroughly disordered lifestyle can destroy normal sleep. If you stay in bed till noon one day, then stay up to the early hours of the morning the next, you are confusing your own body clock. No matter how long it was before you slept, get up at a regular time every morning.

One problem is to identify the cause of insomnia. Early morning waking can be a symptom of depression, which needs medical help. Occasionally, it is part of a pattern of heavy drinking. Waking in the middle of the night can be caused by pain from arthritis or rheumatism.

An evening routine normally helps people get to sleep. Make sure that you do not discuss upsetting matters late at night, or watch too compelling a TV movie or work too late. Give yourself three hours to wind down in the evening. Develop a night-time routine — clean teeth, potter round the bedroom, last hug, lights out.

Sex is nature's way to a natural sleep, provided that it is loving and affectionate. Some women have no desire for sex during the withdrawal period, but then surprise themselves by feeling strongly sexy afterwards.

101

Husbands who have tried not to push themselves on to an unwilling wife who was withdrawing from pills may find this sudden enthusiasm rather surprising. Most will be delighted. Do not be afraid to take a tactful initiative in lovemaking. Even if sex is not on the bill, a last-minute cuddle is very good for inviting relaxed sleep.

If you still can't sleep — accept the fact. Worrying about it will make you feel worse. Expect some tiredness for the following day. Sleep will come eventually.

If you still need help...

If after trying these methods of living with anxiety, you still feel uncomfortable and anxious do not despair. Some people find that they simply cannot put good ideas into practice without the help of others.

Sometimes a self-help group offers this kind of aid. If not, it may be worth asking your doctor if he can refer you to a clinical psychologist. Clinical psychologists — not the same as psychiatrists — have a range of techniques, treatments for anxiety. They will offer relaxation techniques, treatments for phobias, and help in analysing your anxieties. Unfortunately there are not many in the National Health Service, but persist in looking.

Some women feel they need help in sorting out their lives once they have stopped their pills. Once again, their doctor may be able to refer them to group therapy or to a psychotherapist. Avoid encounter groups, weird types of treatment, unqualified psychotherapists and religious cults. They can do harm.

Some fringe medicine treatments are harmless, even if they are not proven to be good. Osteopathy, acupuncture, and homeopathy help many, though some conventional medical experts feel they are quite unreliable.

Basically, it is best to use them for fairly specific problems. Osteopathy or chiropractice will help with back trouble and joint pains — but is no good as a treatment for depression or anxiety. Some women find acupuncture helps them stop smoking, but it is unlikely to solve major problems in a marriage relationship. Try to fit the therapy to the problem.

Avoid those who make inflated claims or charge inflated prices. Fringe medicine has many ripoff artists.

Finally, remember that each and every day that is free from pills is a triumph. The good days are there to be enjoyed. The bad days are there to be lived through. But any day without a pill for a person who was once dependent upon them is a celebration of the human spirit.

TEN

Dependence in Family and Friends

Tranquillisers and sleeping pills can sometimes affect women's lives indirectly. If somebody close to you has become dependent on these pills, their behaviour may be affecting your life. A drug-dependent person sometimes behaves in an odd way.

Recognizing the problem is not easy. You may well feel that something is wrong, but not be sure what. Some women do not link their partner's odd behaviour with the fact that he is taking tranquillisers. They may even feel that in some way it is their fault.

Others cling to the belief that the drug must be doing good — somehow; after all, it is doctors who prescribe these pills. Some women may simply never question the drug-taking. Often they do not know what is wrong until their partner tells them. Even then, they may find it difficult to believe.

A few examples

Jennifer — she thought her marriage had gone wrong
Jennifer took months to notice that something was wrong with her husband, Ben. He would not mix socially with anybody, but sat indoors all day watching television and barely speaking.

> He was very self-centred. He clammed up like a zombie. He'd got no conversation. He wouldn't talk to you. And he saw things entirely differently from how he used to....He was off work because of a back operation and at the beginning he took the tablets like painkillers. It made him different every day. It was terrible really. I didn't know what to expect....I knew he was on one or two tablets, but I didn't know the amount he was taking. I though the marriage had gone wrong. I was threatening to leave him. Then he told my mother he was on these tablets.

Ben came off the tablets abruptly, because he did not know otherwise. He suffered from agoraphobia and other withdrawal symptoms. Jennifer would arrange to go out for the evening, and then Ben would say he could not face going out.

'It was hard to understand at the time. I said things I shouldn't have said. But then we began to understand what was happening. He used to talk a lot about it and I would wonder how long it was all going to take.' But slowly Ben got better — and so did their marriage. 'It's like it was before he started taking the tablets. We can go out together. I'm so glad he's off them.'

Harriet — *she told her husband not to stop the pills*
Harriet found it difficult to recognize her husband's problem

> I suppose in retrospect he was different from the man I married when he was taking them. It seemed to be more and more difficult for him to survive and lead a normal life....He wasn't forgetful or bad-tempered. He was frustrated. When he didn't take a tablet, he felt bad. He got so that he knew he couldn't live without them. But the problems he had originally needed them for were no longer there....My husband's a fighter and a couple of years ago he said that he'd got to find a way to get off them. We discussed it all through. In the beginning I used to say to him 'But the doctor says they're helpful. You'd better keep on with them.'...You see, we didn't really think about addiction. The word 'addicted' never really entered our minds. It wasn't until we found a self-help group that we even thought of it.

Helen — *they talked it over*
When Helen's husband Sam became dependent upon tranquillisers she could feel the difference.

> He wasn't the same person that I had married. Before he went on the pills he would go out and about to dinner dances and meals out. He was a very outgoing person....When he first took the pills it wasn't too bad. But then later he would say he did not feel well enough to go out. We would have arranged something, but then he didn't want to go....He wasn't difficult to live with — just depressed, with bad headaches all the time. I felt so sorry for him. It was no good saying 'Pull your socks up'. He couldn't.

All I could do was to try and keep calm and happy through it.

Helen had a good relationship with her husband. They talked about the problem, and he decided to give up his tranquillisers. She offered her loving support through the time of withdrawal.

Theresa — she recognized drug dependence

Theresa was lucky. About the time she took up her relationship with James, she had become a member of Alcoholics Anonymous. She had realized she was an alcoholic and with AA's help she had stopped drinking.

In AA, she met women and men who had not only been alcoholics but had also used pills. Some of them had become dependent on tranquillisers as well as alcohol. Theresa therefore knew that some individuals could become dependent on these drugs. James did not drink, but he did take tranquillisers. Theresa began to suspect that he was dependent on them.

> I could see that James didn't realize it. The drugs seemed to affect him physically rather than mentally. I had been going out of my mind with alcohol, when I was drinking. He never drank, but the pills he took made him feel ill a lot of the time. He didn't know why. He also had terrible fears....In AA I met people who had also been addicted to tranquillisers, and who had had withdrawal symptoms coming off them. Then James tried to cut down and he had a terrible time.

Theresa recognized the withdrawal symptoms that she had been told about. 'By that time I'd met an AA member who was also a member of Narcotics Anonymous. I introduced her to James, and he went along to NA. I noticed his attitude changing. As we went to the meetings he began to see that he had been addicted.'

Elderly parents and pills

When the person whose pill-taking is causing you concern does not live with you, it is even harder to be sure about the problem. Elderly relatives often live on their own. If your elderly mother or father seems to be getting confused, forgetful, senile or depressed, it is well worth checking what pills they are on.

People in their over-sixties should be on half doses of tranquillisers or sleeping pills. Sometimes special small doses are recommended by the manufacturer. Consult the dosage chart on page 25. Those over the age of eighty should not be taking these pills at all.

Sometimes, because of repeat prescriptions, the elderly are still on the doses that they were taking several years earlier. A dose that did them no apparent harm when they were in their fifties may be far too high ten years later.

The situation is complicated by the fact that many elderly people are on more than one drug, and may be very muddled about which drugs they are taking. One eminent British doctor tells the story of an old lady who had been prescribed eight different kinds of pills, each with different instructions. Her daily routine was to take one from each of the separate containers, shake them all together in a jar, and then take out four at random for the morning, leaving four for the evening.

A survey carried out recently in the homes of elderly patients discovered that nearly two-thirds of the old people had not seen their doctor when their last prescription was given out. Those who were taking over-the-counter medicines admitted that their family doctor probably did not know about these. It has been estimated that at least ten to fifteen per cent of the old people admitted to geriatric wards in Britain are there because of illness produced by drugs.

Elderly relatives, therefore, may be in rather a muddle about their medicines. You can help them by asking them to show you all the pills they take. Make a note of the type of drug, the dose and how often it has to be taken. From this you can work out if they are on too high a dose of sleeping pills or tranquillisers. You can also find out if they are taking too many different pills.

It is not enough just to warn them about it. Elderly people are sometimes very anxious about their doctor, and may well simply do nothing rather than confront him. Sometimes they are just very sensitive to any kind of disapproval —

and doctors *can* be disapproving.

Besides, it is particularly dangerous for the elderly just to stop taking the pills. Even reducing the dose may affect them. They need proper medical treatment, and sometimes hospital treatment. It is often said that a geriatrician's real expertise lies in knowing how to take old people off their drugs — rather than given them new ones.

Offer to go with them to the doctor, and explain your fears when you are there. If they are not happy about this, then ask them if you can go and see the doctor without them. *Never* bully or push them. Do not do anything without their consent.

Denying the problem

Sometimes a person who is dependent upon drugs will deny this. Indeed denial is said to be a symptom of some kinds of drug dependence. These denials, sometimes subtle or sometimes in the form of outright lies, are often found among drug addicts and alcoholics.

Everybody knows about the drunk in the cartoons. He comes back late at night stinking of whisky, barely able to stand, and tells his wife: 'I just had a couple of drinks'. Hard drug addicts may lie in the same idiotic way. So far not enough is known about tranquilliser dependence to know if this denial is often found among women and men who are dependent on tranquillisers or sleeping pills; but it may well be.

The point about these denials and lies is that they are not just wickedness. They are one of the mental symptoms of the disease of drug dependence. The dependent person dare not recognize his problem. He lies about it or denies it in order to persuade himself that nothing is wrong. Sometimes the drug dependent person is literally the last person to know about his problem.

You may therefore find that people get angry, upset or even positively outraged if you mention the possibility of drug dependence to them. This is a sign of their inner fears and a symptom of their illness. If you recognize this, you are less likely to become upset yourself.

How can you help?

If you have a warm and loving relationship, then it is probably worth trying to discuss the problem at least once. Pick your moment carefully. Choose a time when both of you can be relaxed and in a good mood. Speak quietly in warm loving tones of voice. Never bring up the subject if the person is too drugged to think clearly.

Tranquilliser dependence is such a newly discovered problem that some sufferers may have no idea that it is even possible. Explain that you have been reading about how people accidentally get addicted to tranquillisers and sleeping pills. Tell the person that nowadays experts believe these drugs should not usually be taken for more than six months at the most. It may be helpful to lend them this book.

If the person you love simply denies that there is a problem, drop the subject for the moment. Nothing is gained by nagging, bullying, wheedling, or coaxing. This will just give the drug dependent person an excuse to think: 'My wife nags me so much that I *need* tranquillisers to cope'.

Alternatively they may admit the problem, but say that they do not want to give up the pills. Difficult though this may be for you, *accept their decision*. If people try to give up their pills when they are not really wholehearted about the decision, they will probably not succeed anyway. To get well from drug dependence, the addict has to *want* to stop taking the pills.

It is sometimes said that a wife cannot *cause* her husband to become an alcoholic, she cannot *control* his drinking, and she cannot *cure* him. These three 'Cs' apply to drug dependence too. It is not your fault if your husband has become dependent upon pills. Equally, it is not your duty to *make* him give them up.

Self-help groups

Some self-help groups for people coming off tranquillisers welcome husbands and wives to their meetings. Others keep the meetings only for those who have a problem with pills. There are also special self-help groups for the relatives and friends of those with a drinking problem (Al Anon, for example), and those with a drug problem. If your partner mixes alcohol with pills then the former may help you.

Much depends on the degree of disruption that the drugs are causing, not just in your partner's life but, through him, in your own. Sometimes family life is distorted when one member of the family becomes dependent on a drug. Thus not only does the dependent person suffer, but so do the other family members. In this case, the partner of a drug dependent person may need help and advice himself or herself.

Besides, people who become dependent or addicted to drugs often relapse back into that dependence. Cigarette smokers often give up smoking — only to go back on cigarettes either months or even years later. Alcoholics are also prone to relapse into alcoholism. We do not yet know if tranquilliser dependence will show the same rate of relapse. If it does, then this adds to the stress in the family of the dependent person.

This strain can be reduced if everybody in the family remembers that drug dependence is an illness. The dependent person did not choose to become dependent. It is his misfortune, not his fault. Much of the worrying behaviour of an addict is a symptom of the illness from which he suffers. It helps if you can think of the dependent person, not as weak-willed or bad, but as a person with a mental and physical illness.

Helping others to recover

If your partner, relative or friend, decides to come off their tranquillisers or sleeping pills, you can help enormously. Love, affection, encouragement and, above all, patience are what are needed. Constant reassurance and encouragement is the best thing you can do for them.

I got enormous help from my husband,' recalls Margaret, whose story was told in Chapters 5 and 6.

> I hung a chart on the kitchen wall, which showed my progress. He and the family used to make encouraging remarks about its progress....My daughter was a tower of strength to me. I used to go round and sit there in her house all day saying nothing.

I don't know how she put up with me, but she did. She was wonderful.

Helen's husband, Sam, says: 'I couldn't have carried on reducing the pills without her. You've got to have somebody who understands what you're going through. I got very agoraphobic, and I couldn't go out without her.

Do's and dont's during recovery

Don't get too emotionally involved in their progress. The decision when to come off pills and how fast has to be theirs. Be patient if they lapse, or seem to be making little progress. You cannot do it for them.

Do be prepared for withdrawal symptoms lasting quite some time. They are not exaggerating them. Some people have very few, but some individuals have a very tough time indeed.

Don't take over all their duties and chores. People withdrawing from tranquillisers need simple chores and activities to keep them from brooding. Don't leave them with nothing to do.

Do help them get to self-help meetings. In the first weeks of withdrawal they may not be able to drive or cope with public transport on their own. Take them to meetings and attend with them, if they want you to. If not, respect their desire to be at the meeting without you. Help them get there nonetheless.

Don't be upset if during the withdrawal period they don't feel like sex. Sexual desire and enjoyment will come back when they are feeling better.

Do help with agoraphobic fears. Take them for short walks. Accompany them on shopping trips. Slowly help them get used to public places and people.

Do listen. They will probably want to talk about their drug dependence. What they say may be harrowing or just immensely boring. Sympathetic listening is the kindest thing you can give them.

Be prepared for your own reactions

Be prepared to feel some emotional upset yourself. For

years your partner, relative or friend, has been living in an artificially tranquillised fog. Now they may erupt into all kinds of feelings — anger, crying, irritability, panic attacks, even bursts of euphoria.

All this will be a wearing experience for you, too. You may well 'catch' some of the emotional turmoil in the home. Don't be too disheartened or dismayed if you get upset or even occasionally angry yourself. Just say sorry and start again.

Sometimes the person who has come off drugs goes through a period of obsession, when he tries to reform the world, change the medical profession, and stop anybody else taking the drug. This overriding obsession will settle down into more balanced behaviour in time.

Helping others is also part of recovery. When the addict helps others, he makes good use of his former addiction. Many self-help groups are organized round this idea — that the helped person becomes a helper in his turn. The idea is that this helping others guards the addict from relapsing back into drug dependence.

Once again overactivity in this area will usually settle down, as the addict recovers. Remind yourself that over-involvement of any kind is better than the former drugged dependence. In time, a balance will come.

Some partners feel jealous about the close relationships in self-help groups. If you have spent time trying to help somebody off drugs, it can be disheartening to see others succeed where you failed. It is dismaying to hear somebody you love parroting the remarks of others. Try to overcome this jealousy. What matters is that the ill person is getting better.

A new relationship

Sometimes a marriage has existed for years with one partner in a state of drugged dependency. Tranquillisers and sleeping pills seem to damp down emotions, making people artificially submissive and quiet.

When people wake up from a dependence upon pills, their emotions come to life. The comfortable groove of years may be disturbed. For years Mum has been content to

112

cook the meals, tidy the house and do what the family wants. Suddenly she gets ideas of her own.

Alternatively it may be Dad who has the tranquilliser problem. For years he has been quietly sitting in front of the TV saying very little. Now he has come off pills he may begin to reassert his authority in the house.

At this point the family may have guilty feelings about it. 'Maybe he was better when he was on the pills. At least he never interfered then. Now he's busy laying down the law all over the place,' is how they feel.

These reactions are natural. Acknowledge them to yourself, but try not to act on them. If you need to, get help from outside the family. Confide your difficulties to a self-help group, a priest, a counsellor, or a sympathetic friend.

Sometimes a marriage or a partnership has to be renewed again. The relationship has changed and the change needs working through. This can be painful. Marriage guidance, which is given to unmarried or homosexual couples as well as married ones, can be helpful. Comfort yourself with the thought that a changing marriage is at least a living one. Dead marriages do not change. On the whole it is best to wait until the withdrawal symptoms are over, before starting counselling. A person going through severe withdrawal symptoms may not be able to cope with painful insights.

If your loved one stays on drugs

If your partner, your friend or your relative refuses to come off the drugs, or relapses back on to them, you have the hardest task of all. You must admit to yourself that there is nothing you can do.

Accepting that you are powerless over other people's behaviour is not easy. But that is the truth. Nobody can force someone to give up drugs. If the addict does so temporarily, then he or she will probably just relapse back again as soon as possible.

Bullying, coaxing, wheedling or arguing are likely to backfire. If you pile on the pressure, the addict may well retaliate by taking more of the drug. Do not make threats — unless you are completely prepared to carry them out whatever the consequences.

Yours is a very difficult role. All you can do is practise loving detachment from the sick person. Do not get emotionally involved in what is *their* problem. Do not try to stop them taking the drug. But do not protect them from the consequences of taking it. If you make it easy for them to continue, by covering up for them, you are only encouraging the dependence.

Treat them with kindness and love. Never forget that drug dependence is an illness and a misfortune.

Look after your own life. Make sure that the joy, the interest and the happiness you need is in your own life. Find it among friends, at work, and self-help groups, if you can no longer find it in your relationship with the drug dependent person.

Stay hopeful

It is painful, very painful, to see somebody you love suffering in the grip of drug dependence. It is heartbreaking when you seem them recover, then relapse back into their illness.

Do not lose hope. There are thousands of women and men who have managed to recover from drug dependence. Sometimes it has taken more than one attempt. None of us can control another person's life. All we can do is stand back, and wait for them to decide to get well.

APPENDIX 1

Barbiturates

The barbiturates are powerful drugs which used to be prescribed as sleeping pills and sedatives, and are also used in the treatment of epilepsy. As sleeping pills and sedatives they should no longer be prescribed, since they are highly addictive and dangerous in overdose. Nevertheless they are still sometimes given, mainly 'by elderly doctors to elderly patients', as Professor Malcolm Lader says.

Barbiturates include the following: amylobarbitone or Amytal, amylobarbitone sodium (Sodium Amytal), butobarbitone (Soneryl), cyclobarbitone calcium (Phanodorm), heptabarbitone (Medomin), pentobarbitone sodium (Nembutal), phenobarbitone, quinalbarbitone sodium (Seconal Sodium). There are also two compound barbiturate drugs known as Evidorm and Tuinal. Two other drugs, which are not chemically barbiturates but act in a very similar way, are glutethimide (Doriden) and methyprylone (Noludar).

Barbiturates have a place in medicine for the treatment of epilepsy and in anaesthesia, but they are *not safe* as routine sedatives or sleeping pills. If you are on these drugs, ask your doctor to help wean you off them. If you are not willing to do this, at least change to the benzodiazepine family of drugs. Being drug dependent is never healthy, but it is safer to be dependent on benzodiazepines than barbiturates, as far as we know. After changing drugs, try to follow the instructions in this book and attempt to come off benzodiazepines.

Self-Help Groups

This list of self-help groups or contacts was compiled at the end of 1983. Groups may have moved or ended since then. New groups may have started.

Please remember that all groups are short of money, and of help. *Always* send a stamped and addressed envelope, pay for literature and make a donation, if you can afford one. If possible try to help others through the group in your turn. Only by doing this will help be available to those who need it.

Self-help groups for tranquilliser problems only
Tranquilliser Withdrawal Support
160 Tosson Terrace, Heaton, Newcastle, NE6 5EA.
This group may move premises in 1984 so check with telephone book. Mail, however, will probably be sent on.

Tranx
Joan Jerome, c/o 2 St John's Road, Harrow, Middlesex, HA1 2EZ.
Tranx is also planning to move in 1984. Check with the telephone book for new address.

Tranx Release
P.O. Box 1378, Sheriff Street, Dublin 1.

Tranx Release
Jane Bristow, 106 Welstead Avenue, Aspley, Nottingham
Tel: 0602 760550.

Tranx Release
Mike Morledge, 81 Peveril Drive, Ilkeston, Derbyshire
Tel: 0602 304287.

Tranx Release
Anita Gordon, 14 Moorfield Square, Southfields, Northamptonshire.

Appendix 2: Self-help groups

Groups for people with a drug problem — tranquillisers as well as other drugs

Narcotics Anonymous in London, Bristol and Weston-Super-Mare. P.O. Box 246, London SW10.
Tel: 01 871 0505.
NA is spreading fast and may well be in other major towns by the time this book is published.

Other groups which may help

If you are mixing pills and alcohol, you can get help from Alcoholics Anonymous. Check in the local telephone book or write to Alcoholics Anonymous, P.O. Box 514, 11 Redcliffe Gardens, London SW10
Tel: 01 352 9779.

Families Anonymous is for the friends and relatives of those with a drug problem.
Families Anonymous
88 Caledonian Road, London N1
Tel: 01 278 8805.

If you cannot find a nearby group or contact...

Check with the local telephone book or directory inquiries under 'Tranquilliser', 'Tranx' or 'Tranx Release'. Ask the local reference library, womens' advice centre, Citizens Advice Bureau, local group for mental health, or any group offering advice on drugs.

If you write, with a stamped addressed envelope, to MIND, 22 Harley Street, London W1, they *may* be able to help. Because they are researching into tranquillisers, they may know of new groups.

Failing this, the local Alcoholics Anonymous meetings might help. AA has regular 'open' meetings where non-alcoholics are welcome. You may find an AA member who has come off tranquillisers at one of these, or at least pick up some tips or support from others. Much will depend on whether local members are sympathetic.

Starting your own group...is a possiblility, but get well first. Take advice from established groups before you decide. Don't rush into it.

Useful books
Sound Sleep, Dr Quentin R. Regestein with James R. Rechs, New English Library 1983, has questionnaires to help you work out why you suffer from insomnia — useful if, after withdrawing from the drugs, you still cannot sleep well.

Stress and Relaxation, Jane Madders, Martin Dunitz, 1979, has relaxation exercises to do at home.

Trouble with Tranquillisers is a pamphlet produced by Release about giving up tranquillisers. Send 60p, including postage and packing, to Release Publications, 1 Elgin Avenue, London W9 3PR.

For information about drugs and pregnancy
Foresight
The Old Vicarage, Church Lane, Witley, Godalming, Surrey GU8 5PN.

Index

Acupuncture 102
Addiction, LBC programmes in 44
Agoraphobia 105, 111
Al Anon 110
Alcohol 47
  abuse 24
  addiction 55–6, 63–4
  and tranquillisers and sleeping pills 33–4
Alcoholics Anonymous 62, 64, 79, 106, 117
Alexander Technique 93
American Food and Drug Administration (FDA) 19, 31
Anxiety living with 91–103
  methods of reducing 91–2
Ativan (lorazepam) 4, 29, 61
Attitudes, altering 97–9, 100–1

Barbiturates 115
  and benzodiazepines 6–7
  Sodium Amytal 52
Benzodiazepines
  comparison with barbiturates 6–7
  definition of 4
  how to use 18
  as muscle relaxants 89
  value of 13–14
Body relaxation 92–5
  exercise 93–4
  meditation 94–5
  techniques for 93
Brand names, for tranquillisers and sleeping pills 8–10

Caffeine 18, 101

Case histories
  alcohol addiction and pills 55–6, 63–4
  helping others, 53–4, 60–1
  housewife 51–2, 58–9
  insomnia 52–3, 59–60
  pill abuse 54–5, 61–3
  pills without problems 50, 57–8
Chlordiazepoxide (Librium) 4, 6, 54, 56, 57
City Road Drug Project 49–50
Clinical psychologist 102
Clobazam (Frisium) 29
Clonazepam (Rivotril) 10
Coming off tranquillisers 72–3, 84
Committee on the Review of Medicines 19, 26, 49

Dalmane (flurazepam) 4, 28
Data Sheet Compendium 26
Day-at-a-time plan 79–80
Deep breathings 93
Dependence on tranquillisers 38–48, 49–56
  in family and friends, 104–14
    continued 113–14
    denying the problem 108
    emotional reactions 111–12
    how to help 109, 110–11
  as an illness 39
  physical 40–1
  psychological 41–2
  recognizing 45–7
  size of problem 44–5
  vicious circle of 42–3
Diary, keeping 88

Index

Diazepam (Valium) 4, 6, 9, 17, 20, 21, 33, 54, 70, 71
Doctors
  enlisting help from 65–7
  helpful 67–8
  unhelpful 68
Dosage chart, for tranquillisers and sleeping pills 25
Drinkwatchers 92
Driving and tranquillisers 27–9
Drug
  addict, image of 37
  dependence and abuse 49–56, 61
  psychotropic 5

Elderly 24
  and tranquillisers 35, 106–8
Euhypnos (temazepam) 28
Exercise 93–4

Family, dependence in 104–14
'Floppy infant syndrome' 32
Flunitrazepam (Rohypnol) 47
Flurazepam (Dalmane) 4, 20
Frisium (clobazam) 27

Halcion, (triazolam) 43
Hangovers, tranquilliser and sleeping pill 11–22
Housewife, and pills 30, 51–2, 58–9
Hypnotics 4–5
Hypnovel (midazolam) 10

Insomnia 52–3, 59–60, 88–9, 101
  'sleeping pill' 42–3, 47

LBC addiction programmes 44
Librium (chlordiazepoxide) 4, 6, 54, 56, 57
Lorazepam (Ativan) 4, 29

Meditation 94–5
  Transcendental or Siddha yoga 95

Midazolam (Hypnovel) 10
MIND (National Association for Mental Health) 45, 117
mind, relaxing 95–6
Minutes-at-a-time plan 80–1
Mogadon (nitrazepam) 4, 6, 20, 52, 53
Mothers, nursing 24

Narcotics Anonymous 62, 63, 64, 79, 83, 106
Nitrazepam (Mogadon) 4, 6, 20, 52, 53
Nursing mothers 24

Perfectionist attitude 98
Personal care 87–8
Pharmacists 8
Physical dependence 40–1
Pill society 16–17
Pills
  different effects of 32–3
  and the housewife 30
  living without 78–90
    putting drug problem first 81–2
    talking yourself through 83
    telling outsiders 86–7
  and pregnancy 31–2
'Preconceptual planning' 31
Prescribing tranquillisers 7
Pregnancy 23
  and pills 31–2
Problem-solving 97
'Psychic distress' 15
Psychological dependence 41–2
Psychologist, clinical 102
Psychotropic drugs 5

Quaker meetings 95

Relaxing 92–7
  body 92–5
    exercise 93–4
    meditation 94–5

techniques 93
mind 95–6
Rivotril (clonazepam) 10
Rohypnol (flunitrazepam) 47

Safety plan, twelve-point 22–3
Self-help groups 116–7
when stopping tranquillisers
68–9, 85–6, 109–10
Sex, and sleep 101–2
Siddha yoga meditation 95
Side-effects of tranquillisers
26–7, 29–30
mental 29–30
Sleep 11, 101–2
REM 11
and sex 101–2
Sleeping pills
and alcohol 33–4
dosage chart for 25
hangovers 11–12
how they work 10–11
'insomnia' 42–3
international and brand
names 8–10
international consumption
of 5–6
side-effects of 26–7
similarity to tranquillisers
19–22
stopping 65–77
when not in use 13
Smoking 101, 110
Social occasions, coping with
96–7
Stimulants 34
Stress 16

Tagamet, and tranquillisers 34
Temazepam (Euhypnos) 28
Tranquillisers
and alcohol 33–4
dependence on 38–48
as an illness 39
physical 40–1

psychological 41–2
recognising 45–7
size of problem 44–5
vicious circle 42–3
dosage chart 25
and driving 27–9
and the elderly 35
hangovers 11–22
how they work 10–11
international and brand names
8–10
international consumption of
5–6
long-acting and medium-
acting 9
long-term use of 35–6
mental side-effects 29–30
minor and major 4
origin of 6
and other drugs 34
prescribing 7, 12
side-effects of 26–7
similarity of sleeping pills 19–
22
stopping 65–77
and Tagamet 34
temporary effects of 18–19
twelve-point safety plan for 22–
3
when not to use 12–13, 23, 4
Withdrawal Support Group
(Newcastle) 92
withdrawal symptoms 48, 62
Transcendental meditation 95
Tranx 58, 61, 92
Tranx Release 100
Triazolam (Halcion) 43

'Uppers' 34

Valium (diazepam) 4, 6, 9, 17,
20, 21, 33, 54, 70, 71

Withdrawal plan 69–72
from a high dose 72

from a normal-anxiety dose
70–71
from a severe-anxiety dose
71–2
Withdrawal Support Group,
Tranquilliser (Newcastle) 92
Withdrawal symptoms 48, 62
bodily 75

duration of 75–6
mental 74–5
stopping 76
Worrying, for others, 99–100

Yoga 93
Siddha meditation 95